THE Golden FORCE

DR. EARL W. BLIGHTON

Holy Order of MANS
Corte Madera, California

Copyright © 2012 Holy Order of MANS All Rights Reserved
Published by Holy Order of MANS, Corte Madera, CA
HolyOrderOfMANS.org

No parts of this book may be reproduced in any form or by any electronic or mechanical means, including information retrieval systems, without prior written permission from the publisher.

Cover photo: John Towner/Unsplash

Cover and interior layout and design by Carolyn Oakley,
Luminous Moon Design + Press, Boulder, Colorado
luminousmoon.com

First Edition
First Printing: December 2021

ISBN-13: 978-1-7370176-6-0

Publication Data
Dr. Earl W. Blighton
The Golden Force

Religion: Mysticism — Religion: Religion & Science — Body, Mind & Spirit: Alchemy, Mysticism or Spiritualism — Body, Mind & Spirit: Mindfulness & Meditation

Printed and bound in the United States of America

Other Publications by Holy Orders of MANS

Keystone of the Tarot with Meditations
Tarot 22 Keys — The Major Arcana (tarot card set)

Forthcoming

Jewels of the Wise: Self-Mastery Through the Tarot
Stars of Heaven

DEDICATION

This book is dedicated to those who seek the Light in order to make a difference in their lives and their world.

The Golden Force

Acknowledgments

Keeping this book "alive" and available to readers since it was originally published by the Holy Order of MANS in 1967 has been successful due in great part to the unfailing perseverance of Helen Blighton, wife of Earl W. Blighton, the author. By the late 1980's the Holy Order of MANS came apart. Special thanks to Mark and Mary Anderson of the Science of Man, which created a website in the 1990's, and under the direction of Helen Blighton, some of the Order books were made available online. Special thanks to the hundreds of Order members who made it a point to keep copies over the years of all of the literature of the Order, which included this book. Special thanks to those who continued to do the Work of the Order. Special thanks to Mary Ray for retyping most of the Order literature, a daunting task, in the mid 1990's and putting it on the website HolyOrderOfMANS.org. Special thanks to Margot Whitney, Director, Holy Order of MANS who, in 2012, resurrected the Order for the 21st Century. Special thanks to Carolyn Oakley at Luminous Moon Design for her patience and talented work designing and laying out the book and cover. And thank you to Michael Maciel, Director, Holy Order of MANS, for his contributions toward the publication of this book.

Most importantly, and with heartfelt gratitude, we placed our trust in God.

"…and Jesus looking upon them saith, 'With men it is impossible, but not with God; for with God all things are possible.' " (Mark 10:27)

The Golden Force

Introduction

The Energetic Function of a Self-Realized Being

"A scientifically controlled study conducted by German researchers at the University of Kassel in 1997 has shown that while the chest area of an average person emits only 20 photons of light per second, someone who meditates on their heart center and sends love and light to others emits an amazing 100,000 photons per second. That is 5,000 times more than the average human being. Numerous studies have also shown that when these photons are infused with a loving and healing intent, their frequency and vibration increases to the point where they can literally change matter, heal disease, and transform negative events."
– *The Power of the Heart*, Grace MacLeod, gracemacleod.com. Reference: *Case Study: Visible Light Radiated from the Heart with Heart Rhythm Meditation*, Puran Bair, M.S.

The process of spiritual awakening begins with understanding a few basic concepts, and how to apply them in everyday life. This book tells us how to do that and it does it with the exuberance and plainspoken style of the great master teacher Earl W. Blighton.

While spiritual enlightenment cannot be taught, how to get there can. That's what *The Golden Force* does. It gives us the basic understanding of a few key principles that enable us to live fuller and more productive spiritual lives. It opens the door to understanding why we need to develop the spiritual skills of focus, concentration, and meditation. *The Golden Force* allows us to awaken to the great cosmic being in which we live. This path is The Way, with the direct practical application of the power, force, and energy of God.

The adversarial position of science and spirituality was created through a loss of first-hand knowledge. It can be gained back again by experience and imagination. The partnership of science and spirituality is instrumental in regaining our position as co-creators with God in the evolution of mankind.

The Golden Force is written to wake you up to your potential. It awakens people's concepts to consider the way they live: do they create their lives, or do their lives create them? The point is to understand the experiences you're having, why you're having them, and what to do about having more of them, and less of some of them!

We're taught that *God is All One*. And yet, we have a dichotomy of *you're over there, and I'm over here*. Both statements are true. Try to imagine that. The mind can't grasp this. The heart can know this, though. *The Golden Force* is written alchemically to trigger inside your mind little hints to get you to this place where you realize that you're whole and you're in charge, and you're responsible. And you can handle anything thrown at you. It opens your heart.

Spirit never changes. Your soul is wrapped around a small Star, Spirit, at the center of your being. We've arrived in a physical body to fulfill the experiences needed, as determined by our soul, which will allow us to see this Star. In the night sky you see the Milky Way of stars. The Star residing within you is the Sun of your personal solar system, which is your body.

The Golden Force gives us the ancient mystery teachings in today's language, the language of practicality, science, and experience. After all, what good is spiritual knowledge if we cannot put it to use, moment by moment, every day of our lives? This book shows us exactly how to do that.

The Holy Order of MANS is an organization dedicated to a more thorough understanding of the universal laws of the Creator, so that all might better manifest God's Creation and thus promote Peace and Harmony among people everywhere. Our purpose is to teach the Ancient Christian wisdom to this new generation as it was taught in the past.

Our organization is called the Holy Order of MANS because the universal laws of creation, the law of prayer, and other principles can be taught and, in your everyday life, you can become the master of your fate through conscious application of these principles.

We use the term "man" to include both men and women.

The Golden Force

The Golden Force

The Mover of Mountains and Man,
The Builder of Stars and Planets and Seas,
And Servant of Man;

The Golden Manna of Flame and Fire,
Is the Word made Flesh.

Emmanuel
(God With Us)

The Golden Force

Contents

Dedication v
Acknowledgments vii
Introduction ix
Holy Order of MANS xi
1. Man and His Atmosphere 17
2. Man and The Universe 31
3. Growth 37
4. The Law of Psychic Unfoldment 47
5. The Golden Force 57
6. The Marriage in Peace 65
7. Universal Law of The Creative Mind 75
8. Forgetfulness—The Way to Christ—Be Christed ... 83
9. The Way of The Son of Man 91
10. The Ocean of Sex: God—Man—Woman 99
11. The Blind Man Sees 111
12. Consciousness 119
13. How Much Do You See? 127
About the Author 135

Emily Hoehenrieder/Unsplash

Chapter 1

MAN AND HIS ATMOSPHERE

It was a bright sunny day in San Francisco and I was strolling down Market Street. Not having lived in San Francisco very long, I met no one that I knew, but it is a friendly city so I enjoyed the sunshine. The streets were not crowded, so when I passed people, I did not have to scuff and slide by those I passed.

Unconsciously I came up close behind a lady, close to her—within several feet—when she turned suddenly and looked directly at me. I had made no sound walking, as I had on rubber-soled shoes, and there were the other sounds around me, the shuffling and clicking of heels, which were all so natural and would not attract anyone's attention on a busy street.

I walked on down the street wondering at the directness of the look, and tried to remember if I had seen this lady before. No, I was sure I had not. I also remembered having had this happen before. Surely this has happened to you many times—maybe you have not questioned it.

This incident of mine on Market Street is a perfect example of the unconscious transfer of the vibration of one person's atmosphere into another person's atmosphere, when the two atmospheres intermesh or come in contact with one another.

The foreign vibration of one transferring or being felt by the other tells the person there is a stranger around. How does it do it? Well, it acts just like having an infrared lamp turned on your back or any other place where you did not see the source of the light, but felt it. This is done through the electromagnetic field of one person being picked up by the other.

Let's use another example of the atmosphere's function. Have you ever interviewed people for jobs or work where they will be going to play a certain part in a company, or church, in which you are working?

A man stands before me; we have never met before. I personally know nothing of the fellow as to his background or history. He came to me for a job—this is our first interview. I am at my desk. He is standing just in front of it, until he sits down there. Somehow though, there is a personal feeling, an attraction, which seems to be stirring inside of me. I like this fellow. Why? He is five-foot-eight, about forty, with more or less nondescript facial features. It is true he looks straight at you, but some people have developed this attitude toward people. He does not have a look of high intelligence, but I like to be near him.

We may size up a person, or try to find out "what makes him tick," who may live in the same club or hotel or apartment house. Each person thinks, at least subconsciously. Thinking is a process, which produces and causes electrical waves of vibration—electromagnetic waves—to radiate from the brain and physical body. Whether we know it or not, this is a scientific fact. It also is a fact that as we think we build up in space around the physical body a vibratory pattern which we call man's atmosphere (and it really is).

The description above is the nature of your personal atmosphere that is felt or sensed consciously or unconsciously by those we meet, and with whom we associate. This is why I liked to be near the young man on our first interview.

This is your atmosphere and every day in every way you are forming your atmosphere (and what will be in it) through which people must approach you—also all the things that you will experience, and by this we mean the people you are going to draw to you. Then there are the things such as money, houses, cars, clothes, etc. And the things that put you in touch with these whether they can be accepted in your body—that is, aside from their chemical content. Then we have our personal reaction to colors, which are entirely our own reaction to them, for each person even sees colors differently. This has been proven in the selection of shades of colors by several people, and then calibrating their selection on a machine, which has no past to affect its decision. This atmosphere is also part of your protective mechanism in this atomic age, with the fallout of atom bombs and all of the other changes that are taking place.

This atmosphere is formed from your thinking, reactions to things that happen in this life of yours and its events, as well as those things you bring over from the last lifetime. There is also a certain amount of the prenatal period experience, which goes to make up some of your atmosphere, and which reflects in the soul thinking.

Thinking and action—the conscious or unconscious acceptance of these and other things such as race, religion, national philosophy, childhood events, environment, etc., form part of the thinking pattern and acceptance which changes your atmosphere. Let us not forget the real name of that which affects most of our thinking, **mass mind**, which is the composite pattern of what society wants to accept—also wants us to accept, true or untrue—as they say, "hook, line and sinker."

These all go to make up your atmosphere, or, as some think of it, your nature, but really it is the atmosphere around your body, as the air we breathe is part of the atmosphere of the earth. A person versed in astrology believes this atmosphere is determined at the hour of birth. Let us say here that the stars impel or make easier to happen, but do not compel, as man has free choice.

In short, a tide of circumstances first met you, through incidents of many lives. And thus entering this life cycle, you have a certain amount of things which go to setting up certain potential reactions—a part of a predetermined pattern of known causes and actions which also necessitates some thinking in the general understanding of life and what you are relating to, such as money, work, morals, etc., in whatever vein of thought or action your karma lies, in order for these things to be possible to appear in your life.

Jesus asked the people to "Repent and *forsake* their sins." The base word of *repent*, if you will stop and think—the word pent means "stored or confined within a certain boundary." The prefix *"re"* means to reverse the action or in this case, to release. Thus to "Repent and forsake their sins" is to release and leave behind their errors and not to continue to carry them along through life. Some people will tell you, "It is a pretty heavy load I carry," and so they struggle on in their martyr pose. For you are a recipient of the present-day *martyr* complex if you do this.

This is not predestination, but depends on the action which is within your power to change and control. It is within the power of every person to do the right, wrong, or negative thing. All of these go into making up your atmosphere through which filter all sound, thought and reactions, through which the power of God manifests in your life. It determines what shall come into your life, as the God Force will be patterned in accord with the contents of your atmosphere and your acceptance.

Therefore, every person builds his own atmosphere through his thinking, action, the words he speaks or thinks, and previous action. This is what is generally thought of as his individuality, but is a lot more potent and serious in its far-reaching effect. It is your atmosphere—your personal **universe**.

If this were the only truth connected with the subject, it would be of little concern or interest now to continue along with this line of study. With a correct understanding of the Universal function of the teachings of Jesus, and many of the other Great Masters, one may change his or her entire life.

Let us go further with our idea of education in terms of specialization as they do in colleges today—to discipline memory, and train minds to follow one specific groove or line of science. It is true some certain subjects, such as a language, mathematics and history are taken by all. But are our students taught to think? Then, because the student being turned out is so highly specialized in certain subjects and because our technology has reached out into visual space, we are apt to deceive ourselves in thinking and learning of twenty years ago, and that this method should give us a brighter future for our nation as a people. But was this training for the **good of all**, or was it for the benefit of a few, special privileged persons?

The real good of a man to himself and the good of the community and his country are what his atmosphere along with the others' atmospheres will create as a nation, as a world. What comes through the masses of independent atmospheres thus becomes the **mass mind**, which controls the thinking and has control of the masses and what they accept; also, the acceptance of a thing such as the laws we ask our law-makers to pass, to control our movements, our associations with others, as to being right or wrong.

Then there are the unwritten laws of our societies in different countries. These laws are really not legal but they are the ones, which say you send a card of thanks to your hostess after spending a pleasant evening in her home; also the many other business ethics which are generally observed that are accepted by the masses and therefore become part of the mass mind. But because these are accepted does not mean that they are right or wrong according to the Great Creator's Law and Order of the Universe. Then this pattern of forces becomes the ever-impounding influence on the sub-conscious mind, whether you know it or not. This is what people must free themselves of in order to freely work with the Law and gain the God Consciousness.

It is very much like putting oneself in a huge sphere made of a transparent plastic—the plastic being of paper thickness, which has been treated in a way to allow just certain light rays to pass through. This would be similar to the use of a filter on your camera. When a person wishes to take a picture on a bright day, or if he is interested in bringing out certain details in a picture, he uses a certain type of filter. In other words, only certain waves of light can pass through because of the filter, thus certain things in the picture will be stronger and others weaker. The filter is your atmosphere.

The question then is, "What kind of atmosphere has the college built in the student's personal atmosphere?" The college itself certainly has its own atmosphere in which the student remains for four years; and the teachers and teaching body have their atmosphere—the pattern which has been set for teaching and the repetition of the teaching material—these all go to build a distinct pattern. All of these have decided effect on the atmosphere.

Also, the nature of the atmosphere is determined by the response to pattern of itself and its motivation. In other words, this atmosphere will determine what a student will be able to conceive when he is ready to go to work—conceiving the fundamental ideas for his company or employer for which he is being presumably hired as an Engineer, a Scientist, a Designer, or a Salesman.

The question in my mind is: If the student leaves college taking with him his new atmosphere, is he going to hold out any and all theories which were not commonly accepted by his college in the books, which formed the course of study to which his atmosphere is now attuned at this time? Will he hold out new ideas not taught in the text he has studied? Is he not simply adrift on a sea of noncorrelative and unscientific thought? By unscientific thought we mean contrary to the Laws of Nature of God, for after all, are we not functioning in the Mind of God and is not this Universe a manifestation of the Great Creative Mind of this Solar System?

Therefore, anything that does not take into consideration the Great Creative Force of the Universe—can it have a positive functional lasting good? Anything that is not working positively for the evolving creation of God—how can it live and last in the mind of God as a living science?

Now don't look around and say that all this murder and evil, or negative action, has lasted for thousands of years. Remember that this time element is only a man-made point of consciousness.

Is there a safe anchorage to be found for this new worker? Does he have the tools to cope with this unspecialized world of God, in which he must live and create? Let us see if he can start out and use what he has attained in school or must he re-adjust himself to the unknowns of the research group and what we call experience?

This atmosphere of his—the atmosphere of all of us, whether we go to college or to no school at all—is of the greatest importance. It is a mighty reality and through its vibrations must come the things that you are to receive. Though it is not understood by most people now, in this new age it will be taught as a fundamental part of the mental science. Undoubtedly it will be taught in more scientific terms, but we will have solved the problem of living. Its existence is as real as the noonday sun. We feel it every time we mingle with people. It sometimes attracts people good or bad—sometimes it repels. Sometimes its reactions are felt stronger than other times. It is the medium of two lovers. If you want a man in your life, put one there—the one that would be right for you or the one that you want; but you cannot accept a mate and reject this mate at the same time, as some have tried to do. Just as long as he is not already spoken for, he will come to you. He will also stay if you are capable of measuring up to this man of your dreams. This holds true with anything—be sure you are adequate to be with, use or afford whatever the item may be.

When recognizing an unfavorable atmosphere surrounding a friend or associate, we attempt to change it. As a rule the results of such an attempt have been a failure; also the cause of much bad blood between people. In the first place it is not the other's atmosphere that needs changing, but ours. Even though we recognize ours should be changed we usually declare, "Well, this is just me so I guess it will remain that way."

This subject has a far-reaching charm that reaches into the Holy of Holies of each and every person, for secretly 90% of the people alive have experienced one or another of these reactions, the sensing of the other fellow's atmosphere, or a psychic manifestation of some sort.

You are not crazy because you function the way God made you. Let a person declare he is ill and he is sure to have what he wants. Let one declare repeatedly and openly, as he has, his inability to control his own atmosphere, and his whole existence evidences proof of his effort to do that very thing.

Does not the very fact that you entertain this thought lead you to ask the question, "Why should I want to even think about changing my atmosphere?" If you have not been successful in controlling this atmosphere of yours perhaps there is a deeper motivation, a deeper desire.

Again, some people have succeeded in their work of changing their atmosphere. Do we not all know people whose atmosphere has been wholly changed—so much so that we were surprised, feeling almost they were not our former friend but some former reincarnation of theirs? How they accomplished this has been explained in many ways. We listen to the many versions but somehow the stories do not bring conviction; perhaps we are pretty well informed in the general knowledge of life. Where is the trouble?

Is all knowledge institutional? Is it that the logic of intellect ever refuses to light the way, or shed light from the source—*The Master Within?* If so, we must recognize a higher guide than intellect to find the truth. *Are you afraid of God?*

In order that we will not be confused, let us start out from this moment forward with a basic infallible Law that will lift the clouds and stop the wavering from one side of the road to the other, regardless as to whether we are Protestant, Catholic, Jew or Muslim. Here it is:

Man controls his own atmosphere, absolutely and without exception.

To prove this we leave the logic of school behind, at least insofar as logic being only applicable to the seen world. We must look within. We enter the throbbing silence of the intuitional with a conscious knowledge of the life-pulse all through us. One cannot refuse to do so, because the statement of our proposition makes it self-evident that

Man cannot refer to the man as seen in your mirror, or the flesh alone. What you will see will be an outcropping of the cause of what and how you built your atmosphere. **Don't forget, you can only see what can come through the filter of your atmosphere.** This inner being is the impersonality of one's own being; it is his unseeable—it is the ego and soul made manifest; it is eternal.

MAN CONTROLS THROUGH HIS CHOICE

This means the true balance with the will made manifest. Thus the true Ego and Will have a way of their own on what the mind accepts, and the *Great Creator* or *Creative Power* of the Universe brings into material being, into your *See (Visible) World – God made manifest!*

Knowledge of power must precede the ability to use the power intelligently. These statements being true, this raises a question: How little does our conscious self-know of the real Self within? This is a matter of the expanding consciousness of man, but we cannot discuss it here, for the purpose of this book is to lead the student to know his Power—not to marvel why he has not known it before—which he will.

It is true that many have learned of a seeming other **God** self to which they could appeal. They did not know the open scientific way to the reservoir of wisdom within; they guessed, and happily, guessed well sometimes.

In these days of power, atomic and other forms of natural power, the return of the *Christ Consciousness*, the new world, the appeal for facts and the need of true balance, the student demands demonstration. It is right that he does. It is well to make note here that the person might even have knowledge of his power and not exercise it. Knowledge of it may give courage and yet all this does not get the work done.

You may know you can learn German because of your acquaintance and discipline in languages, other than the first one acquired at your mother's knee, but such knowledge alone without practice and technique of speech does not give a mastery of even the simplest phrase of German. Reason: from past experience in study

The Golden Force

of language you know what the results will be with faithful work and practice on your part, under the direction of a master teacher in that tongue.

All that reasoning is simple in learning a language. Now how far does it help us in the demonstration attempt? If we can control nothing without the knowledge of the power to be controlled, then this knowledge must precede the use of the power.

From where and whom shall such knowledge be gained? We turn to the Masters of the East and read the marvels done by them and still being done, and yet the story of their unfoldment is hard to reveal to the Western mind.

We look about us, hear of some shining examples of Mastery of self—also of victory won in attaining consciousness by men who could only see to read the bright lights of the advertising. With this hope above the limitless path of **"I can,"** these men have attained their goals. They have touched that one thing which is **Humility**; a state of humility that gave them the use of their power—this power working through them. This is every man and woman.

But this is not a scientific approach and puts one in a state of confusion with indefinite ways to proceed to use of power. It is more a sense of blind faith; nevertheless they won, and this is not to be discounted.

The mind of this modern age of youth is looking for examples of these things which people cannot see or hear with their eyes and ears, to bridge the time/space gap in mind—to take the work out of living. Is this going to be another time in history when youth shall lead the way as it did in the past?

If ever you were in a railroad accident where you suffered severe shock, have you not noticed that for weeks and months afterwards, upon looking on the internet, your eyes would quickly fall upon any item in it relating to or referring to a railroad happening or event—perhaps a disaster. It seemed to you that such occurrences were increasing because you were always reading of them. Today we know your eye was directed to the paragraph by the action of the subconscious mind, from a motive in the nature of a warning. The shock you had received previously made you absolutely still a moment. At that instant the subconscious mind became charged with one thought of enlightening you regarding railroads, whenever it might be on the subject; hence the seeming unconscious action.

The above is good material to build a fear complex into your atmosphere which would limit your freedom. Here too, in knowing of your power through your word, this can be erased.

Here is a demonstration of the fact that in knowing the power accessible throughout words and thought, we must keep all things out of the mind we do not want to materialize, and be still while the subconscious receives the thoughts or patterns of what we desire. This is going to set up a vibration, which will filter out any opposite action from being drawn into our life through our atmosphere.

Here then we find a condition, a state of mind and vibration building into our atmosphere, which has been created by us and any event. To overcome this vibration in our atmosphere one has only to charge the subconscious mind with thoughts of security and peace.

This may be accomplished in different ways but all use the same basic principle. One of the simplest may be to sit alone 10 minutes a day and hold the thought *"I am under complete protection and I am always in perfect harmony with the Universe."* Soon the sitter will find that the stories in the newspapers will no longer bring themselves to the attention of himself or God. In the above case, the action, which produced the condition was involuntary. The action to change the condition is voluntary and scientific; sometimes called by the religionist *treatment*, and rightfully so, for you are giving a new vibration to your atmosphere.

Look over your list of friends for a moment and select one whom you have known for years who never gives a complete and frank endorsement of another person. Though he may appear to have marked tact with the praise of the other fellow, he invariably insists on qualifying phrases by way of criticism. Gradually you observe you cannot come into his atmosphere without being treated to a budget of criticism of others. The others might be friends, or might be public; characters more or less well known. Your friend has learned to pride himself on his wonderful ability to discern faults quickly in those whom he meets.

Soon all his friends know what to expect when they come into his atmosphere.

They too find that within it they are likely to supplement him on the same lines; they too become fault finders. The effect of this on the one who created the atmosphere about himself is to intensify his bitterness, until even they who once listened willingly now withdraw from an atmosphere that has become too oppressive for them to breathe. No one would think it fair to lay this condition to the stars or to environment.

This fault finding is the surest way I know of creating headaches of all kinds and a lack of life force, because the person is rejecting another part of God when he rejects his brother Man.

Many of you will be able to recall a boy who in his early childhood experienced poverty and who, in boyhood, experienced a firm desire to go to college. If a little later that desire became a declared resolve, soon all avenues would open up to fulfill that desire. That desire and resolve created an atmosphere, which attracted the force necessary to draw to him the things, needed to attain the purpose of the young lad.

Many of these young men will tell us that as long as they were consistent and were taking every opportunity and never lost sight of their goal, help came unsought to get them on their way.

With a little reflection, illustrations will present themselves by the score as the causes that may produce this or that atmosphere. This is in accordance with our statement *"Man controls his own atmosphere absolutely and without exception."*

The foregoing now shows that your atmosphere is a product of your thought that makes it what it is, and thought work alone can change it. Although it be true that conditions are started as we have seen—sometimes without any apparent "willing them to be," let us not forget, whether it be the acts and thought of this life span or the last life, or the things that we have stored up in mind before, you are still in command of the direction of the Creative Power of the Father within.

Remember what Emerson said: "Will is always miraculous, being the presence of God to men. When it appears in man, he is a hero and all metaphysics are at fault. Heaven is the exercise of the faculties, the added sense of power."

The atmosphere that marks the strong individuality is universally ceded to be the product of the invisible emanation of thought centered on ideas.

Our proposition as to control of power now reduces itself to this: if we ourselves are master of our apparatus, we know we can control our thoughts and thus dictate the type of atmosphere we are going to maintain in our life—meaning both the material and spiritual living and development we acquire.

Thus we see that our atmosphere is not a mythical principle but a space and time continuum around us, into which we pour the thinking and speech of our living, thus building up a live dynamic force field which is constantly changing as we might change our thinking patterns, and it will or will not permit certain things to come into our lives which we desire or do not desire, according to the thing we have set in our atmosphere.

Call To Duty

From the top of a mountain high
A shaft of light I saw
Sweeping down to me through crags and draws
For as that shaft drew near
The voice of the ages loud and clear
So strong and yet, as tender as a mother's kiss
It told me this
It was the call, oh, so many ages old
That of which so many mystics have told.
If you accept my strength, you must have no fear
Even when great armies draw near.
You must not fear the airway to tread
Out in view, from far and near
The path is steep with no rail to guide,
But the powers of the Universe are always at your side.
No glory of earth can entice or compare
With the feeling of a free-born Mystic fair,
For he lives not on the narrow streets of clay
For his is the Universal Will to obey.

Chapter 2
MAN AND THE UNIVERSE

The old axiom *"As above, so below,"* while old and used in many ways, is still—and always will hold—true as to the relationship of this Universe to all of its subsequent parts therein, both live and living matter and also the mineral world.

The illustration will help you to conceive the relative form and the universal pattern of a universal atom. The atom is not only scientifically accepted as correct as to its being one of the basic units of matter, but also in its action in relation to other atoms, its likeness to the Universe and the movement of worlds in our solar system. These are atoms in the Solar Molecule. **Man** also is an atom in the social order expressing **God**.

Around the earth is the earth's atmosphere and its electrical shell. This atmosphere of earth is the one that holds our air and all the other things that we need to sustain life, so that there it is, when we draw in our breath the giver of life in all its glory. In fact, it is not very well understood as yet by the scientist, although the sages of long ago know it pretty well and used it in healing for many things. The very thing we are talking about is not well understood, that is, *man's atmosphere* and its use and the way of the control of the things is his life. A real understanding of his own atmosphere is necessary; it is so completely and scientifically a duplicate of the solar system and also the atmosphere of the earth.

The earth's atmosphere is also controlled by man. The hundreds of millions of men and women by their thinking produce such a powerful wave of electrical vibration that it fills the earth's atmosphere—which is the mass mind of earth. Thus is the filtering system built up, so that only part of the sun and its rays can enter and reach the earth. As you can see, it will only allow that which the filter will let pass through to reach the earth. That which comes through will be the energy that the people can use and need, as they are advanced to the point of understanding in its use.

It is well here to relate man and his atmosphere to his internal world or system, the system of the physical body. This is done for the purpose of again saying *as above, so below*, what he calls the organic system of the body is also controlled by his thinking. Also the feeding of the cell structure of his physical body—this is fed from his electrical structure, which is the accurate and descriptive name of what some philosophers call by several names: vital body, psychic body, spiritual body, etc. They have a right to call it what they desire.

We have no latitude in which to take privileges. We must stick to the relative scientific name, which is related to its functions. It is a force matrix, which holds the chemical composition of the physical body together and also holds it in a certain form regardless of the supposed aging of the person, or aging process. The electrical structure never changes after the age of maturity. This understanding of the basic body of man and woman is a thought which is and has been scientifically proven if you look for the proof. But like most things, if you do not want to see the proof you won't find it; or if you are determined to disprove it you may come close, but none can force you to accept what you do not want to see.

The understanding of the electrical body of man is likened to when a man wants to understand his relation to God. If he says no, then that is it; but if he follows his inner understanding, then he will so be convinced of his Creator's existence. Remember we said man can create what he wants in his *life*. This is true, try it out. Just toy with the words and say, "Oh that, so many have come before me, why did they not see it too?" Well, there was a Graham Bell, who invented the telephone.

Let us return here to the chemical cells, as they are fed from the electrical structure, and the nature of their function is determined through the energy fed into the cell through the nucleus of the cell. This sets up an attractive pattern so that it will attract the then-needed energies from the blood, which circulates through the blood to rebuild worn out cells and thus rebuild tissue, which has been torn down in work, in play, and in thinking.

The atmosphere that man builds is and does act as a screen for the energy from the sun (son). The electromagnetic fields of the earth are also screened through it. Is this not a wondrous Universe—this body and its own electromagnetic fields? When we look at the simplicity of the laws that control it, there are at least a dozen or two of these, that man clouds his mind with, which are just surplus baggage. In other words, science has certain laws regarding matter but these are for mechanical tests. Actually the basic Universal laws and principles that men use daily are very, very few and these are the only ones with which we are concerned. Now these same few are not in opposition to the scientific formulas, but these laws are simple and allow us to understand man's personal control of the matter in his universe, and what is going to come into it by the use of Mental control or the product of producing certain energy patterns, which are a part of your thinking or else you could not have produced them in the physical world whether you are using chemistry or electro-physics.

Actually all we are saying is that there is a Universal form in this solar system and it is actually the cell, world, or solar system, etc.

It may be there is a greater God of many Solar Systems but in this, my world, it is not important. Now I am concerned with my personal Universe and this Solar System.

I believe that as a man of God I should be interested in learning all that I can about our own body both physically and spiritually, and how to take care of it, for it is a creation and gift of the Father so that we may express His perfect creation here on earth.

These bodies and the control of them as well as the maintaining of a healthy active life, are a part of Self Mastery and the becoming of a Master.

Man and The Universe

The Great One

From the depth of Earth's inner atom
To the towering heights of the stars
From the deepest part of the ocean
To the powerful planet Mars

God moves and has His Being
Surveying His Universe
Aware of each passing moment
Of the creations He gave birth

So man, awake from your slumbers
Be aware of your God-given choice
Soar your thoughts to the sky. Be alert!
Learn to live in God's voice.

For out of each wind's whisper
Comes a voice so sweet and clear
When the birds on the wing, their praises of Him sing.
It's only God's voice you are hearing.

Be thankful for each new daybreak
Sing your praises in the dusk
Join in the ranks for Freedom
Of man from his deep-seated crust.

Know you stand on hallowed ground
Keep your feet and your heart in hand.
Give love to those about you
Be a neighbor to your fellow man.

Chapter 3
GROWTH

Growth is a word with a wide horizon, a distinct Universal Principle. Broadly we are speaking of *mental, spiritual* and *physical* growth.

Growth, as we are referring to it, is an encompassing thing. We are sure you realize that a person cannot grow or expand his mental horizon without gaining a greater spiritual concept. Also, he is bound to have a finer physical development as mind functions easier, and spiritual attainment is not as hard to realize if it is done in an orderly and balanced process.

This is the first step in the movement of man's development into a spiritual Consciousness, which is necessary for him to conceive that there is more to life in this great God Creation than his physical eyes do see.

He slowly learns through self-discipline of his thinking process that he opens the door to the greater and more expansive realms of reality of the world of God. For his consciousness is the spiritual microscope or, should I say, spiritual macro-scope, which lets him see the workings of the greater reality just as the scientist uses the microscope to study the infinite atomic worlds within God's substance.

One may by force of will discipline the thought pattern in regard to the Universal Laws, thus acquiring a fine appreciation of the exactness of mathematical law and any of the social graces. Work in school is good mental gymnastics, if conducted properly with the right premise, and can be the preparation work for higher and finer perception, for true spiritual growth.

One must know where to place the concepts and what one is to hold, also what concepts to disregard—where to place the importance—or they only becloud the intellect; so in attempting the unfoldment of a person on the path in search for truth, a person must be very careful what premise he starts with.

To understand the law and real function of growth, one must remember that the brain is a part—a chemical part, which reflects the God Mind. The Great Mind is reached through intuitive perception, though the term is often used vaguely. In this book it will only be used in its essential sense—as the highest element of the physical Body which reflects the all-existing Universal Mind and acts as a filtering station, directing the impulses of the Great Mind or even the mass mind through the motor system of the body. Even the automatic motor reflexes are reflected through it.

The brain is like a giant glass prism. As the light passes through the prism it is broken up into the various colors and associated with them. Like this, the thought impulses from the Mind and those from the Universal Pattern of the system and method of Body function pass through it and are sent out over the proper nerve system to get the proper function of the physical body. Thus we grow in perfection of function and action in accord with the perfect Universal pattern.

The smoother this path of mental and physical reflexes works, the less disturbance we have from the physical body; also, the more clear will be the psychic or intuitive impressions that come through to us because there is less resistance and less body consciousness, therefore more consciousness on the higher levels of God consciousness.

True growth of Mind referred to is not brought about by storing up historical facts. The question arises here, do we learn any one fact or a dozen facts or do we, in our process and studying, just bring forward to conscious mind the existing facts? Perhaps we should say the informative material only causes us to remember that which is and does already exist in the Universal Mind, thus releasing the fetters or idea of limitation which the mass mind has placed on our thinking. This is the uncovering and bringing to light knowledge already possessed. For ages this has been the problem of the Yogi and many others. If one has a true concept of man and the Creative Force and the unity that binds and holds all these together as one, his next step is to bring himself into the harmonious vibration of that which binds all—the vibrations which bind atoms in wood and steel, and all these different materials together.

What do we mean by a harmonious vibration of that which binds all? Many volumes have been written about this subject but let us sum it up this way: Getting into harmony with God manifesting as the vibrating life force which creates the physical magnetic fields—these are the binders—so, in order to be in harmony with these natural forces, one must first realize that he is a part of the microcosm as well as the macrocosm. You must not feel resentment toward the denser material things which seem to retard your movement and you may not seem to be able to master. You must see it as it really is and the useful purpose it has in the universal scheme. You must feel the closeness of God in this denser form of matter.

This binding action is only made possible through the Unity of Mind with the One Force—**God Power**—in this Universe. All of this power is at the disposal of those who know and use it—the God Force, which works through the chemical laws of attraction and repulsion, which produce the biases. In the chemical world it is this force working through the pattern set at the time of World Creation.

In other words, the atmosphere of the atom radiates around it, and vibration in it causes the composition or element formed by the atom, which determine its elastic reaction and determine whether it is fluid or gas.

Assuming the student has fairly grasped the meaning of the oneness with God—**the Great Creative Power** in life—this very simple statement has taken some people the better part of a lifetime to accomplish, but this is not necessary as there is the key to all Growth; it is a giving over—a releasing the acceptance of intuitive knowledge and wisdom which will come through your atmosphere if you **"let go and let God!"**

Let go and let God—this is the one expression, which after being told to every student who has set himself to know his God and learn the tools he possesses is the simplest and yet the most confusing.

How do we let go? How do we let God? Did you ever come into the house after a strenuous day or an extremely active period of an hour or two and throw down the body in a chair? You just dropped it there—you did not move or fidget, you did not think, you did not take off any of the outer clothing; you just ceased to act or think, you just enjoyed the natural reaction of "no action;" you were just happy to not do anything. Well, this is letting go.

When you really let go consciously you are in a state of not feeling arms, legs, or any other part of the physical body.

Of course when you start to practice this art (and I mean art, for it is a functional part of the everyday life, if you are going to use the tools you possess), when you are going to use scientific prayer, this letting go is a functional part. When you are going to remove the stresses and strains of living from body and mind, here too it is essential. Here is the interesting part, that when you have really let go God will do the rest for the Great Creative Force of the Universe is ever trying to manifest the Great Mind; the Great Mind is ever alert to every pattern that man (its creation) makes. It is the great gift of God—we are told the Father only wishes to fully fill these patterns man makes.

This is the truth, so if you are lacking certain things in your life scheme then you have not made the pattern for them, or you blocked it with another, or did not think that you would have these things anyway. So you did get what you expected—didn't you? Yes, I think you did.

Growth

WORK TO REALIZE GOD EVERYWHERE.

The fact is that once you have built up this atmosphere of yours, it is built to receive and let come through that which you desire. If you have knowingly built up a pattern of joy, truth or desire for truth, health and consciousness, knowing that the Creative Power is in all things—this comes with the feeling that you are not alone and do not face the world alone. This is the beginning of oneness with all that is. You will then begin to express Life, Joy and Happiness regardless of your age, place or money.

We have news for you—you do not face the world at any time; the only world you face is the world of your own being body/soul/mind, and your atmosphere—which is your responsibility. You should prepare them. This is your world and your responsibility.

By silent prayer this is done—not the *"God give me"* kind, but the *"I accept this, Father"*—the knowing that you already have the right to all that is a part of the Great Universal Power, and therefore *It* is a part of your world if you will let it manifest Itself through you.

The first discipline of the person who desires to grow is to make his atmosphere just what he wants it to be—then and then only are the harmonious vibrations going to form into his atmosphere, to form the life and bring the things he wants. Then it will come from the infinite source of power to him—but there must be a complete circuit or things will not flow through his atmosphere. Don't try to help God do this or that—but **let go!**

During the Civil War at the Battle of Chancellorsville, the great Confederate General Stonewall Jackson's atmosphere was broken, I claim, and he, the idol of the Southern Army, whose power over his soldiers had been almost magical and whose fearlessness in battle had carried him safely through a tempest of bullets, fell, never to rise again in the material body as a leader of earth forces on the field of battle.

We speak of this demonstration because it brings forth two points:

One, we know Stonewall certainly believed in the cause he was fighting for, but you see we do not have a personal God Who, because our cause may be right, would adjust our thinking so that the bullet would not hit. On the other hand it might be right for the greatest good. This makes no difference. It is a case where Stonewall's atmosphere had the invincibility pattern which had been set that way all along, but then he wavered and the God Force flowing through the doubt pattern he had now accepted on the day of his death did the work.

This is nothing new as it has many times been said, "As you think so are you." Now this is supported by various authoritative doctors, that at least 70% of the illnesses of mankind have psychosomatic origins.

We now accept the premise that our thoughts produce our atmosphere we desire which will bring to us in our Universe what we want—good, bad or indifferent.

In order to gain wisdom and strength we prepare ourselves to sit in silence each night and morning. At night we go back over the day's events and judge ourselves—not with remorse, but with full knowledge that the events of this day are over—gone. If we have erred we do not accept the error into our atmosphere but we accept the good as far as our life is concerned, and if we have lied or passed misinformation regarding a brother we resolve (if we do) to give the correct information on the morrow. Then we set in our minds the questions we have, and then *wipe our minds clean* with a mental dust cloth and stop thinking and be quiets If some information pops into the conscious mind, we put this down and when we are finished with Meditation, we negate or deny all of the negative things—the errors, the sins, as the Christian Church would say—in other words, we cease to give things any life—then they can no longer exist in this world or any other.

This is true of all things in life we do not want around our world—our personal world. But do not try to govern the personal world of another person unless asked to, and even then not until you have really perfected your atmosphere to a state of greater perfection, if you are a new student in this endeavor, for you can get in trouble and greatly disturb the other person.

The art of meditation is not concentration. This is entirely used for a different purpose. We will speak of this later. Before going into meditation we must remember first, we are going to break away from the mass thinking or mass mind so that we have no dogmatic principles to follow.

There is but one Mind and one God, a God that does not wear pants and is a great sentient Force. Therefore *It* does not care what your religion was in that *It* did not originate any of the things you call Church. Some of the works of the Great Ones have been left out of the Christian Bible and that is why it is necessary to have no barriers or superstitions. There is no personal God sitting in a material heaven on a material throne welcoming good immaterial souls to this material heaven and with equal justice sending immaterial souls to a material hell full of fire, fear and hatred. My, what a lot of friends I am going to have there.

Growth is impossible with such concepts of being. For the proof of the Truth, science and an understanding of the continuity of life exists, and the proof of life on other planets exists, for many who pass through transition from here go to other worlds to live and grow amongst a higher race of development. The idea of hell and old heaven is being buried by the **truth in science of scientific facts**—in an unmarked grave where it will never be unearthed by the fear mongers.

Emerson says: "I am the oldest Religion. Leaving aside the question: Which was prior, egg or bird? I believe the mind is the creator of the world and is ever creating; that at last Matter is 'dead' mind; that mind makes the senses it perceives with; that the genius of **man** is a continuation of the power that made him and is creating through him."

Assuming then that you have awakened or have never been enthralled in that nightmare of ignorance, and that God or Being means to you above all Intelligence: that within this Intelligence is substance—the Creative force of the Universe made manifest—and that you are one with that Creative Force; and that you are an atom in the composition of this Universe. You must understand why it is your right and necessary privilege to come into harmonious vibration with all the other atoms, which are affected. The absolute Creative Force of this Universe is flowing—you to it and it to you. God gave Man dominion over all the earth. "You are on the Earth." You are Man.

Don't you see—you are seeking only what Creative Intelligence gave you. Your possibilities are limitless. The only price demanded is tireless effort of knowing. You are asking how to *know*—how to take the *Almighty's* free gift to yourself.

Let us not forget that all we ask is—let us lead you to the treasure of Universal Mind, so you may make it all your own, as it is already yours in the first place. The Universal Mind is also your storehouse of Knowledge, as well as the source of the things you seek. Through it you get your needs supplied. All needs are different but they come from the same storehouse through the same channel which bring ours to us. "The Way is a straight and narrow one" but brings *freedom*; yet being narrow, it has limitless width and boundless dimension.

If you are to surmount self—know your birthright—your oneness with God. Your way to limitless supply is through a proper vibratory pattern, established in your atmosphere through a control of thinking, and secured by the knowledge of the **Law**. This will attract the people and things you have accepted. You might say the Way of Faith was laid open—in other words, the width and breadth of the Knowledge you have attained. **You know God or Creative Power** will bring what you have accepted and that your atmosphere will make it possible for it to come through to you.

Spinoza said he affirmed that when man is self-conscious, that is, when he is aware of his own existence, then God realizes Himself, "For he that glorified My Creation knowing first that I created it, to him shall the secret of the Universe be revealed."

If you are one with all creative force, all power is yours. Hold the **truth**—assert it and forever banish every devil (evil) from your consciousness, and your atmosphere will allow only that to come to you which you have accepted.

"This mighty (**I am**) Impersonality" we cannot define, but yet this infinite force we can appropriate. Hardly have we started to perfect our atmosphere by meditation, right thinking and scientific prayer than the true vibrations begin. We cannot force the pattern, what we want to be filled, but the truth of law and order and harmony flows through us; for by knowing, they will produce it for us.

Let me say here—Peace and Harmony are the outgrowth of the discipline of mind and lots of work. The use of the Law and the much talked-of Peace and Harmony (which cannot be studied) will become a **reality** in your life when your atmosphere is cleared. Oh, how true the word, "For my yoke is easy and my burden is light."

Dollar Gill/Unsplash

Chapter 4
THE LAW OF PSYCHIC UNFOLDMENT

The progress made in teaching in the last fifty years is a worthwhile accomplishment in human endeavor. The pupil no longer tries to follow the long and tedious task of learning verbatim the thousands of books in history, civics, etc., but he is learning to associate needed facts with other correlated material. He is being prepared to associate with other people, maintaining better relations or at least a more tolerant mental attitude about their views than he would have had in the 20th century upon leaving college.

The question of what is the process of study or learning is that each person is an individual and has his own profound understanding of how he can absorb the new knowledge, if he does really absorb anything at all and if anyone really understands what the learning process is, in this wonderful Mind of ours, or is it my personal mind? Perhaps it is ours; perhaps it is your mind and my mind and the Father's together. The subject of learning is deep and profound and it leaves room for erroneous moves—because you, your neighbors, the community and the country are going to live with the result of your acts and mistakes.

Some might say it is a modern trend of things in general, but when one stops to think about learning it might be the methods have been changed—which are methods of communication—of the students, but really have the natural processes changed? Does man and his thinking function basically differ from that of fifteen years ago?

Does man's psychic part of the brain have a new and modern process, or is it the same as that of the Master Jesus when he was here? Did he have a better mind than you have, or was there something he did that we have not been taught to do? How was it that, at twelve years of age, he knew things he had not been taught by anyone? He played as a child at games only, but with adult thinking. **Perhaps there is something the dogmatist did not want us to learn—why?**

We will speak of this later, but the prime function of association of objects and things is the same basic principle there as it was in primitive man—although we have in this age, with an awakened psychic consciousness, a more evident function of this facility and thus do not rely on memory and just the things we have read or studied, whether we are conscious of it or not. These correlative methods of obtaining knowledge are most closely related to the true form of our nature and mean that which will function in accord with the Law of the vehicle we are now using—this body and brain.

Varied and diverse reasons may be assigned to the basic cause for this improvement. In part it may be attributed to better facilities and better teaching material; better equipment is being used, also teaching is now no longer a "sissy" job but is respected socially, if not financially. The teacher is certainly not going to get rich on his present-day income but as a whole we believe it is followed by those who love to teach and love people.

Let us say here that a student cannot go through school, even now, without working for it. There are many things which one could attribute to the consciousness necessary to have adequate communication between the teacher and student, for there must be a distinct consciousness on a certain level of exchange between these two in order that there be a good communication on the academic level of the projected material of any subject.

Taking all of these into consideration, we personally believe that back of all is a function and law of psychic force, and that other body which science has not fully accepted—the Psychic Body of

The Law of Psychic Unfoldment

Man—needs a great deal of study and observation on the part of our scientist, in all branches of science which may be related to the species of man. Although the ancients have for thousands of years accepted and taught its function with regard to health and the acquiring of knowledge through its function, modern man knows little of this, the same as he knows little of **God** or why he is here.

Let us see if we can discover it, this **Law** of control. At the commencement of the semester in school in autumn, the good student will observe that it usually takes him some time, maybe ten days or so, before he prepares any lessons to his complete satisfaction. In fact, they seem anything but a part of himself—they are foreign to his whole personality—there is not the least blending between him and them. Even though he may make a good record in class he knows he has been repeating information he has gathered—not presenting knowledge, which he has made a part of himself. In a short time the blending begins—lessons are more easily mastered and he has entered into friendly relationships with his foreign surroundings and acquaintances. Would you say this is a natural result of careful study, and that is all? If a natural result, there must be a cause—a Law. Within that law there may be volumes that ought to be lodged in our consciousness to make it an automatic part of ourselves.

Right here another fact is to be noted, that is, that orderly students have fixed hours each day in which to prepare each lesson. This is not a thing for study alone, but also for prayer which has been done for many ages past by many great sages.

If we were to ask this or that one why he selected one hour for study as against some other hour, he probably would say he did not know the reason—he would say he began the term that way and kept it up. Each student would feel that the plan he is following is best for him and this is undoubtedly so.

We talk too much about unconscious mental action. Even some of our writers do not seem to recognize that subconscious mental action is anything but unconscious action. It brings to us the highest intuitive

The Golden Force

knowledge. To distinguish between conscious and subconscious thought is to take a long step toward the attainment of the wisdom of the ancients. The student, in selecting the hour for the preparation of his lessons, is usually directed by subconscious thought action. He always is when he finds that hour especially congenial for the particular work assigned him. The psychic Law, we are trying to tell you embraces within itself both time and method, which in reality is form (meaning shape or pattern).

The pattern or shape is the procedure and idea, of how the student accepts that he is able to study, how the studying will be most easily done to relate the subject to him or her, for they are people of a distinct experience which no one else has ever had or ever will have, for they would have to become him or her. Therefore, his or hers are unusual experiences and they are unusual people, in that they are this particular reflection of the Great Creative Force now reflecting Itself in matter at this time, in this particular way. It is God reflecting Himself in their experience.

In some cases the selection of the hour or time for work on any particular study may not be of serious importance. If the student comes to his work with a heaviness, as though he were wearied before he starts, not much of anything can be of help to him, for he is tired. He'd best sit quietly, sit passive and accept strength and peace and harmony in his own Universe first.

When he has been refreshed and is back to normal, no longer weary, then place in the mind the question as to the hour he should select for the task of studying his assignments. Of course, it is necessary to first get himself really quiet and then the steps are as follows:

1. Sit relaxed and at ease, not thinking of the next thing he is going to do when he has accomplished this, and he is not ready until he has released all physical feeling as much as possible.
2. Then ask his question and be sure he himself makes it clear to himself what question he is asking himself—do not slough

The Law of Psychic Unfoldment

it off as a thing he is already conscious of, just because he is asking the Higher Intelligence within (whom he probably has not consciously contacted before). Make the question clear.

3. Then he takes a clear, clean mental cloth and wipes off his mind, so he has no thought impressions left of anything. Then he sits quietly, patiently, and the answer will come to him. Often the answer springs forth in such a manner he will ask "Who said that?" Sometimes he may hear a single word, "now!" We are all more or less aware of the spontaneous answers or questions. Have we been conscious as to their origin? This is the way the Intuitional speaks to us and through the inner consciousness. Let the student learn to trust it. The hour selected rightly, let him remember that the Attainment of Knowledge is not a cramming process. He is not trying to learn how to use what is in books—but what is already in the Universal Mind, there, here, everywhere. In other words, what he reads will stimulate and bring to the surface the wisdom from within him, from the Universal pool of wisdom and information in the Great Mind.

If the student has not been an investigator into the science of the seen and unseen, then I would suggest that he try this science of the Universe—try this method and see that it works for himself. It would take more space here to adequately explain it and many of its ramifications than I have allotted to the entire book. But this little rule will work as it is.

There is one point to be clarified here: when you are reading any book of this nature, which relates to the person and his progression, whenever you come across the word *development*, remember it is not development you seek but the unfolding of your memory: thus it is *unfoldment*. It is the unifying of one's self with the basic force of the Universe. We are not talking about some great power or deity in some far-off place. We are talking of the basic power of everything—the you, the me, the force of creation made manifest in and through the life force; the force behind the atom, and the thing that causes the atom bomb to be so destructive. Then, are you going to say, "God did this?" No, not the way you are thinking, but it was the power of God, released by **man** in a certain direction, which wreaks so much havoc, just as in so many other things man uses the wrong thing or the wrong way, or he gets himself in the way by not listening to the whole truth, and wants to have his own way.

No one adds a new power to mind, but simply brings to active realization the latent powers one has always possessed. Remember, this does not require you to be a saint, or wear a long white beard and long white robe. It does not mean that if you successfully use it and are successful in your experiment with this intelligence that you have become a Disciple of the **Great Master Jesus** or on that level of development. You can use it and still be the meanest man in town; it has nothing to do with whether you are good or bad, only you cannot be indifferent and use it.

Learning of the Power you possess is not a dry and uninteresting task. Far from it—it is an exciting adventure. It is the new frontier for most people. It is a frontier of boundless, unlimited horizons with a new and beautiful world, which was created many eons ago by the Great Creative Mind, God—or whatever you wish to call it.

Let me repeat correctly, it is a frontier of boundaries unknown, with boundless opportunities, unlimited horizons with a new and beautiful world. Let us stop here a moment. Why is it new and beautiful, this world; has it all changed? No, it has not changed at all, but perhaps your eyes have been opened and you now see it as it really is, see it with a new color and dimension. Also, maybe you are getting a glimpse of the real world that most people do not see.

Now let us proceed with the rest of the statement, "which was created many eons ago by the Great Creative Mind"—was it eons ago or was it yesterday? Men get to be so important when they think of God.

Sixty years ago, if I had said, "I will have dinner in London with you tonight," your reply would have been, "Just who do you think you are? You know I cannot, it is too far." But you see, our concept of distance has changed, as well as time, for we can have dinner in London that same night.

It is true that time and space are a concept of Man. Time especially is a man-made concept; therefore, maybe it was only created yesterday and in the beautiful world that we are living in and moving through today.

First the student, by his work, creates and cultivates an atmosphere of attractiveness and force, which will draw others to him. It will also draw that beautiful blonde down the block to you.

Virgil, in *The Huntress of the Sun*, in mythology, expands imagination, linking mortals to immortals. The philosopher Cicero's periods bewilder him with their masterly brilliance. He finds himself mentally watching for something beyond the petty seeking for the meaning of words and their grammatical relationship to each other. This puts his mind in condition to receive the vibrations from the ether or memory of nature, which is in harmony with the atmosphere, which he has created, and which he personally accepted to bring the things he desired in his life. The storehouse of nature and God possesses a wealth of experience—the student is seeking and possibly adding some concept thereto, thereby the expanding Universe, the ever-moving *Way*.

However, let us leave the deeper facts for now. To point to the delight in study is what is promised. The student has selected the time to begin the work and understands that change is to be made as to those allotments. Next he is to drop all thoughts of learning difficult tasks, or self-sacrifice about it—he is giving these hours to the unfoldment of the power within. The creative act, wrongly called "work," is now his season of communication with his real selfhood, the real him. Its vibrative force he does not know but is soon conscious of its far reachingness, recognizing it to be infinite force. Instead of learning the lesson, all nature seems to have come to his aid and he absorbed it—not memorizing it.

The Golden Force

The task above is not one of introducing a foreign substance into the receptacle called Mind. Now this absorbed information has become an integral part of his selfhood. He cannot lose it, and though memory has been a function to aid in grasping, the possibility of forgetting is not enabled for an instant. Such an absorption of a lesson occasionally comes to any student without consciousness of it. But if the physical law of the atmosphere and vibration (fixed hours held solely for the special work and study each day are primary requisites) is kept faithfully, such an absorption or assimilation will delight the student and bring to him the joyousness of intelligent unfoldment; these times of effort were formerly many hours of toil.

Remember what Khalil Gibran said in his book *The Prophet*: "Your ears know in silence the secret of the days and nights. But your ears thirst for the sound of your heart's knowledge. You would know in words that which you have always known in thought. You would touch with your fingers the naked body of your dreams."

Even after a successful period of procuring the knowledge on one subject, when you turn to the next one do not falter or fear, for the memory of nature is without depth, and all that is—is there.

With true unfoldment of your real Self and real recognition of this mental unfoldment, which this method will soon bring forth, there can be no possible lodgment of fears, for any fear, which exists at the start, must soon leave. Can you possibly realize and have proven to you that you are a part of the infinite Mind, and still fear the material world about you when in reality you see with your physical eyes so little?

Remember one thing, there are seven days a week, and when you are unfolding your inner intelligence the constant every repetition of this procedure is necessary, until it has become a part of your common functional mentality and you have become fully aware. Then you can turn to it whenever and wherever you might be—in your study, or walking down the street.

The Law of Psychic Unfoldment

Do this seven days a week, so that you will get this pattern into your atmosphere, for the vibration of what you put into your atmosphere is what is going to make it possible for what is going to come out into your life. This will bring to you the oneness of life, your oneness with the Creator of **all life—wisdom of all things—for of yourself you do nothing**.

The Golden Force

Look to the Golden Force
Your ideas will be bright and bold.

Look to the Golden Force
Your pockets will be filled with gold.

Look to the Golden Force
You will never grow old.

Look to the Golden Force
Your future will be bright as the sunrise.

Look to the Golden Force
Your fate is yours to unfold.

Look to the Golden Force
Your service is your armor bright.

Look to the Golden Force
You will be fair for all to behold!

Chapter 5
THE GOLDEN FORCE

In the instructions as to how to use the Psychic Force this question undoubtedly came to your mind: What power of force is this which makes it possible for me to use this method of learning? My answer is—**It is the Golden Force!**

This is the Golden Age in which the real things of the world are to be brought into the consciousness of all people regardless of race, creed or color. The Golden Force is the true gold of the real world.

This is the Golden Age because this Golden Force, this living dynamic power, this unknowable, unseeable, unseen, invisible Force is ever present. This Force while unseeable by humans themselves or outer man (although it is used by them all the time, and always has been used whether they know it or not), is set in motion by them—it is motivated by them. This Force is moved and emanates from a great Creative Mind, not in some far-off Heaven but in everything we touch, use, breathe, say and do.

This is God—It is manifestation which brings into existence our every thought or combination of thoughts and words which are spoken or declared. It is the means through which Man has free choice. It is the means by which our prayers are answered or unanswered. This is not hell-fire and damnation.

This **God**, this Creative God Who created you so that you might manifest **Him**, made you so you could *create*—otherwise you would not be manifesting in *His* image—would you?

The Golden Force

Throughout the centuries past, humans have been looking for the return of a Great Master or Messiah. *He* or *It* is returning to earth—How? Once again the Creator is coming into the consciousness of the people. That is, people are returning to the level and state of consciousness through which they can use this Force of the Creative Mind to solve their problems. Only through its power can they obtain what they desire in their life, and live the full and interesting lives they desire. His people are His means of expression in the material world.

People build their world, as we have said, by building their own atmosphere as they want it to be produced, and bring what they want into existence through their thinking and spoken word. Now look around you and see the world conditions and see what you have helped to build. Look at the murder, theft, rape, and the relations between nations. The relations between nations are nothing more or less than the result of mass thinking of the people made manifest. So if at any time there should be a war or mass rebellion—**Remember**—you are as much at fault as anyone is.

Man can only obtain and maintain peace through a return to God consciousness. In other words, to know that through the **Law, Love** and **Living**, in the consciousness of these three L's and being ever conscious man has the choice, and through his hourly thinking and words, can bring peace of mind and body. Thus will our country have peace, because there is no thought of war in our minds, as war does not come when the individuals are not personally at war with themselves. When the country is at peace, they will not be preparing for war.

The earth will be at peace when the countries are at peace. When one is at peace, one does not have ills.

Peace is not a state of stagnation, but a state of activity in which people are busy creating and letting God come through into material expression.

This is **The Golden Force**, in an orderly ever-changing state of creativity, work and manufacturing, for the use of the people. This is the doctrine of the **Great Master Jesus**.

Man must be at peace with himself, before he can be at peace with others of his kind.

The Creator has not wanted man to suffer nor to be in want. It is only man's ego, which will not accept that Man himself cannot do it alone without the Golden Force, for he—Man—of himself is nothing.

What you put into your atmosphere determines what you will receive.

Man has not been satisfied to create the idea pattern of what he wanted and let the Great Creator bring it into existence through the Law. Once, the Great Master Jesus, said, "It is not my work, but the works of the Father *through* me!"

Man is always trying to control his world through new laws and by ideas of his own, forgetting that the basic *Law* was set down by the Creator when the Universe was created. If man would use this, he could do all things without harm, to anyone or anything.

It is only through *Living*—conscious *living* and *knowing* that we form the patterns in our atmosphere, which the Golden Force fills and brings into existence, and in the pattern of the way we want to live it. Thus we gain the luxurious *living* that the Creator intended for His Creatures on this earth to live, and *not* in *fear* of want in the midst of plenty.

The term *living* is not what we see around us—the existence in fear—bound by limitations, bound by hundreds of conventional laws, *no personal* freedom, no world freedom; and without *freedom* you cannot manifest the Creator, be it in the Atomic Age or now.

YOU ARE A FREE AGENT OF THE GREAT CREATOR!
YOU HAVE THE TOOLS—ARE YOU GOING TO USE THEM—NOW?

The Law

Like studying the atom in a scientific laboratory, the scientist in working on any infinite particle watches its movement, weighs it in a mathematical way and is very careful to see how it reacts to other elements and forces when applied to it. In other words, if he does this, that will happen; and he carefully repeats this process until he is sure he has a thorough knowledge of its reactions. Then he has a basic idea to work on—a basic Law or formula.

Somehow people have reached a stage in this present social period where if they try a way of doing something and it doesn't work, they have a pet phrase, "Oh well, you cannot be right every time!" and then they go on doing the same thing over and over again. This is a tragedy when the thing has to do with life, religion or mind, and things that exist in their community They have acquired a defeatist attitude.

Likewise, we do not see or know God by comparing It with other dense matter, or what God weighs, but through the teachings of many great men—the Bible, the Koran and other great books, and experiences and demonstrations—so we know that a great dynamic Creative force works through the Universal law. As we learn to use it and *know* its nature, we must be just as observing and diligent as the scientist, in our directed efforts, in order that it will work every time—*No Alibi!*

Then again, like the scientist, you know you must control your mental work, and everything must be clearly defined as to the elements you are using in the pattern of matter that you are preparing for the God Force to bring into your world. This is a mental picture or pattern of what you are accepting from God, whether it be a book, a job or a new car. That is to say, the individual must keep thinking clearly and only put into the pattern that which he wishes others to see, as an example of his handiwork, of the things he is thinking.

The way, the road of development of the individual in the use of this Law through which **The Golden Force** will flow, is the thing man is most interested in and, of course, he has it all of his life—know it or not. He has used it unconsciously because all things come into manifestation this way. If he learns to use it knowingly and constructively his observations will tell him his small errors and he will erase them the same as pain can be erased in the human body. The clarity of his results will depend on the clarity of his mental picture, also the clarity of his instructor's mind in his instruction to him.

When reading some things (these were materials in this same trend of thinking) the impression was that the writers were building up this true, simple explanation into a complex thinking structure in order to confuse and confound the reader with their importance. Then again, it is human practice to always confuse the reader or student when they wish to bridge the gaps in their own understanding, so that they will not show.

Simple things are difficult to write about and this is so simple that for thousands of years it has been held, as we say today, **"Top Secret,"** by many of the great groups of Mystics and Occult Orders. This is not to cast any aspersions on them, but it is so, and if you have read the chapters and volumes that have been written on this subject it will help you to know we are not dispensing a new Law and Order of things, but just taking off the Lavender and Lace, so you may get only the essence.

Let me reiterate that simple things are very difficult to convey because there are so few factors or things we have to work with. This is so, for in the realms of nature and Universal Law or Material Law we have but one basic functional operation—the Law of Cause and Effect. There are many ways in which and through which the Great Creative Force of the Universe works, but only through this Law.

The term Law, as we use it, means the step-by-step process which it is necessary to take in order that the Law of Cause and Effect will motivate the Great Creative Dynamic Force of the universe to manifest—bring the pattern and thoughts you put into your own atmosphere, and thus into the material world or whatever world you are concerned with. This statement *"or whatever world you are concerned with"* sounds rather odd, does it not, but let us stop and think—are we concerned with just what we see around us? For if you are a Christian (I am nonsectarian and do not classify myself in a dogmatic group), you should be interested in other worlds. If you are not, you do not believe in continual life after you drop this vehicle or body.

As we have said, this happens every day whether you know it or not and you cannot change it, nor can our great men of science change it; but we can determine what we will receive in our world. The difference in knowing how to use it is that you can stop unwanted things from happening and bring **Law and Order, Peace and Joy into your life**.

You are no longer a victim of accidents, fate or your mother-in-law's law, for her law ceases to have an effect in your Life. You are the creator in your Universe. You can create the things and conditions in your Universe through the Law the Creator laid down when **It** created this Solar System.

When the Creative Energy—God—fills the thought forms in the atmosphere of the individual or group, or the thought forms of a mass of many people, and when they uniformly accept an idea as a fact, **It** controls by the Law, the same which **It** laid down when the Universe was first started. Therefore, all people and things in this Universe and all life and dense matter are under the same control.

It does not make any difference if the person or thing is on this planet or some other, if he is in a physical body or an electrical form, call them whatever you may—spiritual body, psychic body, or what—for the same law governs the integration or disintegration, whether the object is being created or dissolved.

The first and one of the most important things to learn is that the Creator of this Universe does not reach down and set a condition into existence, or create a certain individual situation just because **He (It)** thinks we have earned it—or we should have. We must be of that consciousness that we realize that we are alone, that only through the power of God can we accomplish what we want to with our spoken word and thought. That is, we either use the Law or someone with the same knowledge uses it at our request; otherwise we do not get the results we are looking for. Sometimes we find that a rather "alone" feeling comes over us, but we must face it; we have always been alone but were not conscious of it as now.

The wonderful part of this Great Creator is, **It** will fill our life with joy, pain, health, sorrow, plenty or poverty, and It will do one just as easily as the other. Its only interest is to see that **Its creations are fully satisfied and that their every choice is fulfilled right away, right now!**

THE GOLDEN FORCE WILL PRODUCE IT NOW— KNOW THAT IT DOES!!

What condition is your atmosphere in now? Do you know there exists a **dynamic force in you?** It is the basic energy of all substances; therefore, every cell of your physical and electrical bodies are composed of It. Whether you are in the physical world, or in the world invisible, now, if It is, then do you have your full consciousness of sight? Then you should investigate and find out how to release this wonderful tool the Creator gave you. You can only function by use of this **Law and the Dynamic Force of Creation, for you of yourself do nothing**—except choose, and not stop It from working.

The Creator, **It**, has provided the tools—you create all things and conditions in your personal Universe—it is up to you what you do with them.

Remember, you are the son of God.
You are created in the image of Him!

David Holifield/Unsplash

Chapter 6

THE MARRIAGE IN PEACE

The number six is a good number and it is a good number for this chapter, as it represents a universal principle in the function of things; thus it should have significance here. It is the number of the double triangle, which stands for the function of **Law** on both planes. In other words, it is the **Law** of the triangle in function, on both the seen and the unseen planes of action—in both worlds—in the physical world and the world of **God**, as the religionist would say it, but we say in these two spheres of vibration, because it is really that way. Sounds cold, does it not? Then the student says to me, "Are you trying to tell me that you are talking about a Great Creative Power that really works? You mean a real **God**—?" and it is always to my dismay, for I am sure that I will never quite understand people that go to church, when they do not think that it is a real thing they are talking about. Yes, it is a real **God**, a functioning God!

For years I have been reading about peace and harmony, and how you find this peace and harmony. As I look back, it was summed up in two ways: one was by sitting in silence, and the other was to have faith and confidence in God and develop patience by faith. These are wonderful ideas and both are things that will help in anyone's inner development, this is certain; but does the problem lie in being quiet or having faith? We are inclined to say neither of these are the basic motivators.

The Golden Force

First let us look, can a person be peaceful and still not have harmony? The answer to this, we believe, is yes, for a person can, through futility of striving against a particular thing or condition, attain a certain tolerant point of acceptance with his lot or situation, but this is not harmony. Are you in harmony with a piece of music, or is it that you're not disturbed by it? Many people are tolerant of various kinds of music and sound. Because you do not blow your top when you hear it, this alone is not being in harmony with this particular rhythm or melody.

People eat three meals a day and are still hungry. If they were satisfied fully, they would not want to eat every time they see food. Those who find this situation is existent in their life should look more closely for another reason why they feel this hunger.

When you sit down and rest, are you resting or are you just not moving at the present time? Is this resting? No, it is not moving, but inside of these people they are under constant stress and every nerve is working. In order to rest there must be happiness and understanding of the body they are working in; they must like being in the body that they are in—knowing it is a part of God.

To have peace and be at rest it is necessary to desire to be in the body they are in. For if this is not so, how can they be quiet and not disturbed, so that they may become better acquainted with their Great Intelligence within—if they do not like the house they inhabit? It is a lot like a person with a new car; for a while it is the best car made, but he gets kind of used to it and then he looks around and sees another's new make and right away he is dissatisfied and is no longer at peace with his car. He wants one like Jim has.

Let us look at the book, *The Prophet*. Does he write of Peace?

Answer: No! Many people are like a country, even like the United States. Today we would say we are at peace and that we are working at maintaining peace through the world, but are we at peace? Do we have a unity within our own national entity or boundary, within the nation itself? Are we happy with the governing body of this nation?

The Marriage in Peace

Do we feel that we are one? Do we accept one another as a part of one body united and working together for a common good, or the welfare of all?

This is a slight idea of the blending of form, and force and action in the Universal pattern of things—the way that the unity reaction is in the Universal pattern of things and the reaction itself, and to itself. The question is, do we work in unison as one, or does one take the other along by force? Are you ready to work with the Creator in one concerted effort, without hesitation, and not only half-way? One cannot go halfway with the Creator: It—Creative Mind—goes all the way and so must you. I believe that you will concede that the spiritual ego is one with the Omnipotent Force, and when attuned to harmonious vibrations with the Great Creator, possesses all the Power, its own physical environment and its surroundings, that have been attributed by the theologian to **God**.

This being a correct statement, the chief end of man is to consciously possess the power to bring himself into harmonious vibrations. This done, he has solved the problem of living, sensing God and knowing God.

The purpose, the aim of the student in advanced philosophy today, should be not to learn a new philosophy but to make practical the one he knows to be true. Students are everywhere discussing theories of vibration and the new era, the new age and the Universal Law which governs all matter, all vibration. In short, they are discussing with words—but are they actually working with these fundamental Laws of Vibration? Knowledge of this Law and how it passes thoughts of things through the atmosphere can only reach the intelligence of him whose atmosphere will permit it to pass through.

The wires are laid. You may connect your house or office with a wire and not be able to speak across it; you must have at each end a properly adjusted transmitter and receiver that may give and receive messages across the line. Also you must have a clear mind, a mind that has reached a true conclusion, a conclusion that God comes first in all

The Golden Force

things. You must have reached a conclusion that you, the physical you, are not satisfied with the results you have had so far—by you doing it—so you are going to let the Creative Force work through you.

Primarily, we start with an assumption that all life is one, that all intelligence is bound together by subtle unseen cords on which thought does travel, whether we know it or not. It is not my purpose here to offer any argument to prove the truth of this science, which is so old and so new. Lao Tse, who wrote of Tao, the Chinese God, twenty-five hundred years ago, recognized it and declared that while Tao could not be defined, He could be appropriated. All great thinkers, even Lao Tse and since then, have agreed as to the oneness of life. All advanced thinkers of the present day start with the acceptance of the unity of life, and demonstrate it in a thousand ways, proving the truth of this mighty unity.

Accepting this, then, as true, we as individuals are desirous of coming into that state of knowing, that we are truly coming to know the inner man and the outer man, and that we like the feel of them both—that sense of completeness and balance—and are happy to be with them, and not somewhere else or in an exotic or painful effort to sense their feelings. Happiness is the most profound way—this is what unity means. We hold that the realization of this state of vibration and filling your atmosphere with it, and then the pattern or picturing, which you desire to be created, will cause to come into your world the things that you want in life now, not twenty years from now. During this state of vibration you will establish the connection with the outer world, and your atmosphere will complete the connection, and in will flow the desired things.

With the atmosphere correct, we need only to know how to pray in a scientific manner and the Great Creator will fill every desire and purpose of the mind. This is the gift of the Great One. Let the student remember that all wires are up and strung; all life is bound together by indestructible cords. He is not asked to establish new lines. They were all strung ages and ages ago and they are as universal and eternal as life.

The Marriage in Peace

It is fitting here to state that many times I have listened to the groups of sages and their profound recitals of the wisdom of the ages, and then had them come to me for help due to the lack of the knowledge of how to pray.

Their inadequacy was not caused by insincerity or lack of trying—not at all. You must get in touch with yourself and establish your correct atmosphere in accordance with the world you want, and you will not have hair-raising experiences in the psychic world, or obsessions of a negative nature when you do it, for with this natural process you are functioning as the Great Creator built you to function.

It is peace without a price attached, peace of the most active kind, harmony without sound, sound without effort—just knowing, knowing, knowing, that God and you are one, one, one. No, you cannot take that period away; it is there, for eternity.

Yes, the individual does control his own atmosphere. If you are a slave to the vague philosophy of heredity, environment or the stars, this claim of one's absolutely controlling his own atmosphere may not be accepted by you as by most people. However, we cannot enter into an argument here because I do not intend to be so foolish as to try to defend the Great Creator, and His limitless power of Universe, when basically this is all there is of it. How can I defend my basic Self?

How can you as an individual, as a Christian, as a Jew or as any thought-group at all deny this last statement of mine and still say you believe in the Bible and Jesus' teachings? It is like the hating of the Black, or Asian or Native American, and then going to church on Sunday to teach the Son of God, or however you say it. To me, to get Spiritual Consciousness just from the words in books—it is impossible. It is impossible to be on both sides of the fence at the same time. You either believe in the equality of man, or you do not.

The unity of the physical body and the spiritual or psychic body is a thing that goes on, on and on, because the Law of Cause and Effect, or the positive and negative, are always at work in the world of dense matter, as we call it; or is it so dense at all? No, it is not, if you look at it through the microscope. For instance, the substance of man's body is substance which comes from the earth itself, and when you take something out of the natural pattern of the earth, the natural Law is at work the minute it is removed. Therefore, from the cradle to the grave it is being pulled back to the earth and trying to amalgamate itself to its natural environment in the earth.

You might say that it created you, and we would say yes, that is true. But remember that anything in earth and its atmosphere is a substance that has pattern which is in harmony with the rest of the natural creation of this world, and the wave length and vibration must be in resonance in order to have unity of action through which the Power of God can work and have its being.

Therefore the process of aging is the reaction of natural law at work, in the cosmic scheme of things, in the world atmosphere of ours. The ability to keep from aging is the ability to keep in tune with the source of Creative Power, and so it is essential that you must be in that state of which we spoke in the first part of the chapter, in order that you can transcend the law of nature in this world and become a Universal Being, in that Material Law does not affect you, but that you rely on the Universal law of this solar system, in order to sustain self. Then and then only are you drawing on the central source of power, and when you are through with it, disperse the elements and go your way.

You might say this is some mystical something, but do you believe that man has the power to create? You do? If you do, then you have to admit that he must have the power to disintegrate the same body. This is only just a straight logical conclusion, and we know that all this and all other things in nature are functioning on a strictly scientific principle, and not haphazard way of function. This must be so if you read the Christian Bible, for it says, "He is a just and righteous God." A just God could not work one way with this material or one person, and another way with the other person or substance. There must be a uniformity of functioning in the material Laws or He could not manifest here.

Let us go back to the first page of this chapter in regard to the Marriage in Peace. You have undoubtedly heard of the phrase, "Get yourself out of the way," and "Let go and let God." Well, this previous discussion shows you why it is necessary to have a Marriage of the two bodies in order to have inner peace, for inner peace means that the person has reached the point that he can sit and listen to the inner voice and the Great Mind of the Universe, when he gets quiet enough to let this voice be heard inside.

Let us say that in a specific person this marriage had not taken place, and he tried to do healings on himself. The bodies would not have a concured effort, because they would not be looking to the Great Creative Power for the source of their strength. The atmosphere would be in a turmoil, and although generated by the person to attract a certain thing into his or her world, its potential would be so wasted in trying to overcome the confusion in his atmosphere it would not be strong enough to bring the God Force to him and cause the manifestation to take place.

Once upon a time a man here said, "Love Thy Brother." He did not say if thy brother treated you the way you thought he should, but just plain Love Thy Brother—no matter what he did. This certainly is a large order for us to do these days, when you find it necessary to do and say all things as if you might be beheaded the next minute for fear of having "crossed someone's liver," as they say.

Then we hear someone say, "Well, that was all well and good for him to say that in those days,"—well, be informed that in those days it was not nice.

Back of each of these sayings is a finger pointing at the cause and a means of protection of oneself if he finds himself in one of these situations. The Great Creator never left you coming around third base without a coach on hand to see that you could make it home, and even run a little invisible interference for you if you need it, if you expect it.

He told you to love your brother, because this was putting up the strongest defense that this or any other world could give you. It may

The Golden Force

be invisible, quite true, but the force of the atomic bomb is invisible too. It is the same thing that Gandhi used to free India; it is the force of not accepting anything that you do not want to happen in your atmosphere. Here we have absolutely no fear and no resistance to evil, as you call it.

If you understand this you will know what to do with your bad aspects, if you follow astrology.

If you are a Jew you will understand your religion, and the mysteries will fade away. This takes the mystery out of the mysteries.

No matter whether you are Christian—Yogi—or of any religion or philosophy, there is a way to be Happy—there is a way *to live*.

Let's all live our lives in peace.

The Marriage in Peace

Neonbrand/Unsplash

Chapter 7

UNIVERSAL LAW OF THE CREATIVE MIND

The Creator has provided the Universal tool—**the Universal Law**—and if you really want to produce what you want in your life, this is the way. The following is a step-by-step procedure.

STEP 1

Choose what you want to create and make sure you really want what you choose, meaning—what you really are going to accept.

Remember—the Golden Force is unidentified. It exists in all things; it is the basic substance of all matter. Your choice determines its material manifestation and form.

A person making a choice is like, for example, a woman doing washing. The first thing she thinks of is water. So we in our example use water for the Golden Force. Now, she is going to use three different batches of water: soap water, rinse water, and bluing water. Basically it is all water.

In the first place; she uses soap. The soap determines the function of the water—what action is going to manifest. In the rinse water, she accepts the natural carrying-away power of the water. In the blue water she puts bleach. This determines the action of the whitening of the clothes; thus another action goes on in the same water but it is only through the water that the other elements can be brought together and all of the necessary actions take place to produce a clean white wash.

The Golden Force

The Golden Force will produce any and all things we desire, if we know—**know that it will**. It will open the way for all things.

STEP 2

Become aware that this dynamic force is in you, as well as everything around you—not in some place away from you; and that this Force will materialize that which you have chosen, through the Intelligence within your own being.

STEP 3

Then accept fully this which you have chosen with a feeling of "it is here—it is being handed to me."

Accept it with the same confidence as when your pay check is handed to you. You know you have a check in your hand and that it represents buying power. So does this—only more so. This is really creating the pattern—the real part of what you want.

You are doing the same thing the construction boss is doing when he has his man build a wooden form for a concrete wall, which is needed for a building. The wooden form is the pattern for the concrete wall. Likewise, when you build a mental pattern, which the Father will fill—it is just the same as the laborers who will fill the wooden form for the concrete wall.

STEP 4

Now that your desire has been created in reality and is coming into material existence, **Let go of all thought of it and turn it loose from your mind.** Do not start to think about it or question fulfillment, or look for it; just **know** that it **now exists and you will have it for use as needed.**

Do not question whether it will work or not—stop peeking over your shoulder.... For when you question, you are creating and building a new doubt pattern which the Father will fulfill just as easily as the positive one—only you will not get what you started out to get, or were working for. **Let go! Let go! Leave the vacuum to be filled by The Great Force.**

LET THE CREATOR TAKE CARE OF IT—KNOW THE TRUTH.

Let us take a typical example of what we are talking about. There is in everyone's life the desire to have a car, a camera or a house, which at present wages it does not sound logical that you can afford.

Right here—in the last statement—you pre-determined what **you can afford. This statement tells several things:**
1. That you believe you are the one that makes it possible for you to have a "house," by the power of your earnings which are set by man-made concepts, based on the market demand.
2. That you do not recognize that all "things" are basically of one substance—the Creative Power of the Universe, **It.**
3. That you accept limitations.
4. That you are controlled by **mass mind** at the time you make the statement.
5. That you do not know the working of the **Law.**
6. That you do not know that **It** can only express through you and your brother mankind.

Now, let us know the truth:
1. That you—of yourself—do nothing.
2. That **you** have the right to choose what you will.
3. That **you** can only **earn that which** you can **accept** and to which **you know you have a right**.
4. That **you** have been told that you are what you accept.
5. That **you** can **own nothing**—you may have the use of that which you desire.
6. That **you** are but the prism through which the light passes into a denser form of matter, or into this earth **plane. You** are the expression of the **Great One.** Call it what you may. Do good or otherwise—you are still only able to do it by and through the working of the **Law.**

THE LAW

Man is in a rush to attain material wealth and has closed his eyes and ears to all things which he says are not sound, logical and scientifically based facts.

Right here, let me ask you—how much do you see, really how much do you see, how much of the physical world do you see with your two eyes?

How much do you accomplish with, and of, your own strength?

Let us see what the bible says about this **Law:**

> **Matthew 21:22**
> "And all things whatsoever ye shall ask in prayer, believing, ye shall receive."
>
> **Luke 12:31**
> "Seek ye the kingdom of God; and all these things shall be added unto you."
>
> **Luke 12:34**
> "For where your treasure is, there will your heart be also."
>
> **Matthew 7:8**
> "For everyone that asketh, receiveth."
>
> **Psalm 145:16**
> "Thou openest Thine hand and satisfiest the desire of every living thing."

You will say that, yes, these are in the bible, but this is a religious idea—well, did you ever stop to think that perhaps they meant what they said; that Jesus taught the science of Life and they did mean it?

Universal Law of The Creative Mind

You will perhaps remember the statement, "As a man thinketh, so is he." Well, this too is true.

Jesus also said, "Thy word shall not return to *thee* void." And he said, "Through me shall ye see the face of the Father." The Law is the great formula which the Creator set in the Solar Pattern of the Universe so that His creations would have freedom, one of the most important of all things to learn.

The Law, as we call it—the Law by which and through which all things manifest in this world, or your life—is the process of, or means of, using the Creative Power which brings all things into manifestation. It is the Living Formula of all mankind, whether you know it or not.

The force that we set into action through this "Living Formula" is made up of thought-waves, sound of speech and subconscious impression. These go to make up the combined patterns on which the Formula works—manifestation of our dominant mental and spiritual states.

Shock produces fear and emotional imbalance, which has been known to momentarily cause stoppage or acceleration of the heart. Physicians do accept that under emotional stress, particularly anger, the blood leaves chemical deposits around the joints in the body; and that worry, fear, anger, jealousy and other emotional conditions are mental in their nature, and as such are being recognized as hidden causes of a large part of all the physical suffering to which the flesh is heir.

A normal healthy mind reflects itself in a healthy body. This shows you are relaxed and the Creative Force is working through you. This is the Working of God through the Law, or Formula.

Daily we must control our thoughts that deny the importance or existence of the real, and affirm the presence of God, the Creative Force, in every cell of our being as well as everything that we see or touch. Remember the real is the world we usually do not see, which controls the unreal which we see.

The correction of anything in our life, through Scientific Prayer using **Law**, will work for us to correct body, mind, business, home relations, money or development.

Nothing can keep us from the Love of God. What a comfort to know that all is well with the Soul! Have we not been told not to fear, for it is the Father's good pleasure to give us the Kingdom? It does not specify that it will not work on, or will work on all things—it just says *How*.

The same Force that creates the tissue in the growing embryo in the expectant mother, gives you your paycheck.

What we believe about man, we must believe and accept about God. The Nature of All Universal Being. This is the state of your concept of God.

This determines what you receive, through the working of the Law...

Oh, man, look at your Brother
Do you see yourself or another?
Is this man like you?
Does he show his color in Plain View?
Bless him, for as you bless him,
You bless you.

Free yourself and help your neighbor to be **free** also.

All around you hear the cries about taxes and the **high cost of living**.

What are you doing about it? **Free** yourself through working with the Law and working with your **neighbor**, and **you** will be able to make the Constitution of the United States stand for what it was intended and written for; *a truly sacred document* written by men with great wisdom and vision, who knew man as he really is.

Let us make her the true representative Democratic United States of a World Government, for *all nations*, Indivisible, with Liberty and Justice for all.

By keeping a clear-cut picture of the kind of place you want to live in—**in mind**—**it must come true**.

What you see around you is such a small part of what really is. **This is a scientific fact.** Your physical sight is very, very limited.

DON'T—DON'T LIMIT YOURSELF!
THINK! THINK! THINK!

Tim Mossholder/Unsplash

Chapter 8

FORGETFULNESS—THE WAY TO CHRIST—BE CHRISTED

Oh! Love You, Isn't Love Grand? It is the only way—through the Power of Love. If you have not Love, you are but a tinkling cymbal... We could go on with this line of quotations for the rest of the space allotted to this chapter and still say nothing, just the same as the hundreds of other writings and beautiful words. They are all true, but do you understand what they mean? For years the writer did not, he asked questions of the speakers, learned men of theology, and many other good men, but somehow as the speakers started to answer they always seemed to duck around the corner.

We give you a new-age definition of love, which is what the new age expects of you to do—manifest *Love*.

Do you love this black-skinned girl enough to throw your arm around her and say, "Come with me and we will get you something to eat," and take her into a restaurant and sit down with her and not feel a difference between her and you, and not look out of the corner of your eye to see who is watching you, or if they are? Yes, you will tell me that they are the same, but deep down within you the action of mass mind is taking its toll on your internal reactions. You are not quite comfortable, but do you feel the same as you do toward your own daughter? You are going to say, "How could I, they are not my kinfolk." Remember, you have only one kinfolk and that is the whole race of mankind. That kind of Love is not so easy, is it? For it is Christ's Brand.

The Golden Force

How much do you love the **man** you married, when you come home after a day at the office and you are preparing supper, and he comes over to you to show his affection? Do you say, "Go away, I'm getting supper!"? Maybe you would like to get dinner alone and spend the evening alone. It can happen to you and is going to unless you start to really show the Christ love spiritually, mentally, and physically to your mate. Christ manifests on both planes of action. After all, this is your world, and the things that you disregard—people, facts and things, which you do not accept—will slip out of your atmosphere. Then some sunny day you come to and say, "Where is John whom I lived with? I always washed his clothes and ironed his shirts, and yes, I cooked our meals too. Why did he leave?... Well, I'll get a divorce." —the old favorite. I have news for you—a piece of paper and an allotment check each month is **damn** poor company on holidays and evenings, when you have reached (emotional and mental) maturity. After spending many nights in the bars—good and bad ones—you still have no real friends, except the Great One.

Now this goes for men as well as women, and some of the clomping around some men do and their approach to their mate, in either a mental or physical way, is pretty stupid. Of course they have never been taught in their homes as young men because their fathers or both parents were too busy chasing money for the family. Actually, what the family needed was some real *Love*. The *Love* that says, "I'll go without a new hair-do so John can go to a night class he wants" (or something of that sort).

Love is doing something because the other fellow likes it that way, or it may be that you would *do* something which you might be misunderstood in, but you know that it is for the other person and that you can do no other way or thing because you do love them. Love is the setting of the Law of Cause and Effect into action, consciously, without taking into consideration your personal preference, because of your feeling—your divine relationship with the other person or idea, whether you originated it or not. In other words, you are doing what

God would, if Self could have complete freedom of your body and mind to express here. This is why the Roman Catholic Church says you cannot love anything that does not have life.

There is and has been for many years a spreading of a teaching which cast a lewd light on the relations of a man and woman even when under what some people call the "bonds of wedlock." *Don't you like that word wedlock?* It expresses a lot of freedom, does it not? It seems that somewhere I have heard that to thine own self be true, or you cannot be true to any other man. How true to any other man—how true can you be to yourself when in bondage or wedlock? Yes, you can be true to the one you Love, because when you really Love you will give up anything except your relationship between yourself and God.

With real Love the Christ Force is flowing between you both in the form of the Great Life Force. The male being positive and the female negative—she is receiving strength in the physical sex act if she is a good mate and they are really mated, and there is a real giving out to each other.

We use the term *really mated* because real mating starts in the mind of the two people, and a complete and beautiful interchange of thought exists. Of course the mind is and has its function for the Creative Power of God, which manifests as *psychic force*, and it is given life by using the Christ Force, that is to say, the thoughts and forms of the mind by use of the Christ Force have manifestation in working on the psychic force. This is the way you obtain your sensation for one another.

The relations between man and woman are patterned by and created by God. In the Holy Bible it says that God said He saw it was not good for man to be alone, so He created **Eve**. We just called it the *Holy Bible*, meaning that it is the whole story of man with the exception of the portions of it man saw fit hundreds of years later to take out. If it is Holy, then we had better stick to the story and not deny at least God's intentions and think that we know better than the Creator himself, by calling this relation between man and woman an unholy thing or act—that it is not good.

Remember the ones who decry the Love of man and woman—look close and you will undoubtedly observe that they have been what we call "unlucky in Love." It is a natural truth that misery likes company—don't forget this.

When one starts to tell you in order to become an evolved soul you must give up all of this—all of this evil, this low base part that God created of man, and that this is only for the purpose of bringing children into the world; well if this is true, I know a lot of pretty saintly folks that are going to keep me company in hell. But I am not correcting that statement, for these people are the real creative people on this plan of action and are really manifesting God in action—not just talking of metaphysical persons. They are out working amongst the people in need and people who want to know.

What does all of this mean? It means that in all things we must let the Christ Force work through us and if man and woman surrender to each other with all their Love, keeping the Great Father first, they will know real marriage, the marriage of two Souls through the two Great Forces of the Universe, the **Father and His only begotten son (man)**.

Forget your past and remember the future by keeping your eyes on the light—walk with God and your mate. Remember marriage is made in **heaven**, not in or at the license bureau. Don't forget to Love all men and women, and the last one is very difficult to do.

Look within for the light and be guided by the true answers, if you will let go of all bug-a-boos. Forget your imaginary hurts—that is, most of the hurts are just ego bumps. What if someone did speak a little sharply, perhaps they were not even conscious of it, and what good are you going to get by remembering? Did you have a lover's quarrel? Forget it and remember God, for you will get better results by using your strength that way, and your time is better spent.

Forgetfulness—The Way to Christ—Be Christed

Let the light of God shine through you and the Christ Force give the light of life. It will be a vibrant, dynamic moving beacon of true guidance for the others of mankind. Forget those petty things of your contacts with other people and Love them. Let your Christ Light reach out to them.

Do not carry your feelings around on your sleeve; and remember that you are one with the Great One. Remember that the man of Galilee was no woebegone figure. He was a powerful man of both a physical and spiritual nature. He was Christed—so can you be. There are many people wandering around trying to worship this Great Master and that Great Master, but are doing nothing about the master within.

Our **basic verse** (1 Cor. 15:2) reveals that St. Paul saw the Spiritual psychological approach to life and its "problems" and "related" himself to **"The Christ" (The Divine Self, the Divine Consciousness, "I AM")**—not to his province, or his family, or the year or conditions; thus, he worked from *"That."* A man wanted to have a silence. He said, "I want to hold to 'that' more and more!" Of course, what he really wanted was to "engraft" his "human" attention **into "that."**

We are all by nature friendly and it is our nature to continue to enjoy "people and things," but **first** let us remember to relate our attention to **"that"** which is our **wisdom**, our **supply**, our **immutable joy**.

No matter how beautiful our outer environment—we are supposed to enjoy it and appreciate it, yes, but let us continue to "depend upon" the **soul, "I AM."**

The many conveniences of today and the helpful conditions may tempt us to believe that our "prosperity" depends upon "the time" or "the place," etc., rather than upon **that Individuality**, which is "the same yesterday, today and forever."

When we are "At Home" (consciously) we have **all good**.

"Prosperity—All Good"

Then if we think back as to the old conventional teachings, "The Father, Son, and the Holy Ghost." The phrase that every boy, man, woman and child of most any age can repeat to you, and still few ever have the concept of the true meaning of the words they repeat.

Sunday after Sunday they hear the good Pastor or Priest repeat the words, "In the name of the Father, and of the Son, and of the Holy Ghost, Amen." Little knowing that in these three words lie the missing link to most people's happiness, and strength. If the underlying meaning were to be taught by the teachers, Priest and Ministers there would not be the crime and sadness in the world in general—this, the real basic and spiritual function of the Great Creative Force in action.

The positive **Law**, the thing which the Master Jesus tried to tell the people of when he said, "As a man thinks, so is he," is not this a wonderful revelation? Now you know that by your very thinking you may condition yourself so that your life will be more smooth and full of the things you want and need, and that your physical body will manifest a more delightful zest for movement and action all along the line, and this will be done by knowing that your word will be fulfilled.

I ask you, do you think Jesus would lie? I don't, and I know that what he said was the truth. Do you think that the Great Creative God would put His creations here without a way to cope with the world they live in, to be in want and alone? **No! No!—No!** How could I love a God like that—but did He not in the Ten Commandments say "Thou shalt love the Lord thy God with all thy heart, and with all thy soul and with all thy mind"?

Forgetting old error, start to release the beautiful part of God's creation, for all of what God created should bring joy and happiness to us. What condition is your joy point—Joy Christ Consciousness?

What is the state, or do you have a state of Joy Point? Yes, you do, it is this very moment, for you are not going to be happy the next moment if you are not happy now, or at least decide to be happy. **Now on**—Rejoice, now is a new body, new working patterns, new ideas and above all a New Clear Channel to receive this—A new Life Force.

No sick thought, no poor thought, just boundless strength, health and supply.

First Corinthians 3:16—"Know ye not that ye are the temple of God, and the Spirit of God dwelleth within you?"

Our bodily or personal Universe, the condition of it, is the result of projection of our thinking and our words—our use of the Universal Creative Force (God—Allah) the potential Energy within us, round us. What a glorious Freedom it gives us when we understand that there is but One Mind, the Mind that each calls his own; and that this force through the **Son/Sun** gives us life, joy and love.

The Christ made manifest.

The Great Gift

Not more of Life, Oh Master, do I ask,
But Thy Presence ever near to feel
Not better Sight
But better ears to hear,
But the Cosmic Voice to be ever near,
I need not courage when Thy Presence I do feel,
For I live and have my being in Thy Mind,
year by year.

But one gift do I ask,
This is service with a task.
Never ending until the time
When I leave this earthly vehicle behind.

Then to rest and start anew
To help some other that has but few
Of these precious gifts Thou givest Me,
Love, Wisdom and Charity.

Chapter 9
THE WAY OF THE SON OF MAN

Oh Earth, Oh! Earth! Thy beauty! Where is the Son of God this night? Outside it is raining and it is a much-needed rain. Is it not proof that the Great Law works? The Force, the God Force, works if you will let it. The great power will be in action any time we are sure we are and know that we want this or that.

This night we ask you that age-old question: "Do you really want to know the truth of this Universe?"

Do you want to take the responsibility of knowing? Do you want to use it if you are taught better ways to think? It is better not to know the truth and do nothing than to know the truth and do nothing. For it will catch up with you. And the results of inactivity are not always good for an individual, you will be in turmoil.

Do you want to set your foot on the path of attainment? Do you really want to realize the magnitude of this Universe of the Great God in all His glory? Do you want to reach the realization that the Universe is yours to roam, if you are here in the physical body or after you pass through transition?

"I am the way, the truth and the light," said Jesus. All religions, arts and sciences are branches of the same tree.

All of the aspirations of the whole human race are really directed toward ennobling the being, Man, so that God may be glorified here, lifting him from the sphere of mere physical existence to the freedom of *unlimited Man*—with unlimited power, unlimited strength and unlimited supply of things that he needs for the perfect expression of the Great Creator, here and anywhere, in this Universe.

The Way is a direct path so broad and so narrow that it encompasses man as a being, becoming and relating him to the divinity of all being. It requires certain accomplishments by the individual and certain development of both the physical and unseen bodies with a real consciousness of the tremendous power man has which he was endowed with by the Great Creator.

One of these concepts is the equality of all men and the feeling of amalgamation of him—or herself with the most undeveloped, as well as the highest intellect or spiritually evolved being—regardless of race, creed, or color. This is not just a tolerating of these people; it is the feeling of Love for them and a realization of their divinity. It is the feeling of no difference between you and the man of another race. It is the readiness to put them on an equal basis on this physical plane as well as on the spiritual plane.

One of the other things that must be accomplished is being ready, at any time, any hour or at any place, to give anything you have to give, in time, money and work. Of course you do so without idea of profit, with an eagerness to serve, knowing that "as you do it unto one of these, you do it to me also."

Another one of the things which is necessary for him that would be of service is to be able to teach objectively, no matter what the one you are trying to help says or does. They may apparently leave you in rebellion but you must know that they are in their spiritual being perfect and a son or child of God, the same as the one who is apparently working diligently to change and correct his life.

You must see them, their being, and know that they will return to glorify the Great Creative power of the Universe and become a shining light.

When you are ready to put your foot on the **Way**, you are ready to walk with the tools and work with the tools the Great Creator has given you. **Work** with them and walk the face of the earth anywhere and everywhere among friends or those that think they do not like you, without fear or want. **Walk** in joy and be full of gladness to serve God and man alike. **Walk** toward the point of the rising Son of the Illumination, which gives you the Universal freedom to be in the service of healing and taking of the Christ to yourself, and the bringing of the power within, and thus performing the great function of **Love**—the **Love** of God in all his Glory—the Glory of the Universe and all of the Universal movements of the sphere, which means the controlling of your own sphere by putting into your own atmosphere the shining glory of the Great God. Yet while living on this plane of action, and being conscious of the other world, at the same time of the glory of the freedom, of the freedom to accept a man or woman as he or she is and **Loving all**. And yet see or be able to see the little error they commit without it affecting your feeling toward them. Whether it be a personal and special individual in your life, such as a wife or a sweetheart—and at the same time feeling the love—all Love of the being, as you should feel toward all people. Being able to accept the slap of the dearest one, or the student, and not feel any reaction. In other words, you have gotten yourself out of the way by disciplined scientific prayer. The slap may be a slap performed in many ways; it could be the telling of stories about you, it could be anger displayed to you and it could be a real slap. It might be most anything. The Way is long, the road is steep, the work is great, but the eventide and its thoughts are well worth the effort of the day. The smile of the one that was ill is like harmony of the spheres to you. In it is the motivation for tomorrow, but then it will only be today. Each time you slip just turn around and look, then say, "Well, God, we didn't quite make it this time, but that is finished and done." Once more turning your head to the light, perhaps not knowing just how you will make it except through the power of God working through you, and that this knowledge of **the Law** is all you need because that is all there is to work with.

Look to the light ahead, look not to the right or left when troubled but look ahead, see that one—that man in the dark skin striving ahead

The Golden Force

or the one away in the distance in the shining armor of light, it is and can shine through you also if you will let go and let God be the power and principal force, regardless of what you see around you.

It is the path of the ancient alchemist; it is the path of humility because it is the path of power you see; humility and power are the opposite poles of the Great Force.

We reach the great hallway of time, so to speak, for up to now we have a more or less open road with a limited view, but we see, as from afar off, the Way. As we walk along we seem to enter a long passage in the side of a mountain, and things seem to form a wall, and our path seems to flow into a passageway and I find myself hemmed in by walls, and there is only one way ahead. The way is dim and the light does not seem to come through as it did, but I walk on because I have sighted once the lighted way.

Walking seems more difficult and my friends seem to have left me.

The ones I have always looked to no longer seem interested in me or my welfare, for there does not seem to be anyone ahead and the ones I saw before have disappeared. I am alone.

I ache for someone to talk with in the understanding way, but the ones closest seem to turn their backs. The body is not the springy one I have always known. I have aches and pains and yet they do not seem real, for in the center of my being is a great gaping chasm, so vast it seems to be impossible to fill. Even when I pray, it only brings tears and the flow of the Great Force, which is like a mighty river, but it seems to be flowing into the bottomless pit never to be filled as it was before.

Now I look up, and then what seems ages later I see a doorway, but instead of a lighted doorway it is totally dark. After much travel I reach it, and it is devoid of all light. How am I going to get to the Way beyond—for I feel it must be there. I am certain that I took the right fork in the road back there.

I think and then realize that there is but one way to get my footing beyond. I must have and know that what is beyond is the Way I seek, the path of Illumination. I must step through the door without seeing what I step on. I must know that I have within me the power of choice and the Great Creative Force working through me which will uphold me and sustain me until I am on the **Way** I seek. Oddly enough, the power of the Great God is all that ever held me up all the way along through life. This for sure is all that will ever uphold me and sustain me, now that I reach the **Way**. All that can sustain me on the **Way** is the **Great Power**, the freedom of choice I have.

So I at last pray and reach a decision, knowing that God is everywhere; so I put one foot through the door, cautiously at first, but feel no footing. Then it is that I realize that if I am to be sustained by His power I must release all and pass through the door, without looking backward or without seeing the results of where I am stepping—without a psychic view of the future—or my knowledge of the Power will not work.

At last, after much delay, the die is cast and on the premise of the Great Law I step through the door then, to my surprise, in the full light of day, and I stand with my face to the sun and as I look off to the right and to the left, there is an unlimited horizon.

The Universe spreads off before me! It is a little overwhelming, but I know that the Great One is always at my side, for there is nothing to fear but fear itself.

This is the dawn of the new day. Now I can look along the Way and see there are many travelers on it—men and women, young and old—all with the same happy faces and the same joy in their hearts, and the sun streams down and my strength returns—but *now* it is unlimited.

This is the road of the Masters, not master of others, but Masters of self, for the Glory of God and the fellowship of man. Music now reaches my ears. It is not like other music but the music of the hearts of free men, men of destiny, the servants of **Mankind** who are in the service of the creation of Love in the World, serving with the Great Creative Power—the great God Power of this Universe.

Come, join us, we need more workers than ever before, here are countless millions to serve, millions to heal. Perhaps you are one of them—you shall not go unserved if you ask our help.

This is the new age and the glory of all the Universe is now in the balance, as far as this world is concerned. There is a **Way**; it is not Catholic, Protestant or Jew, it is the **Way** of the Great One.

With this we give you the blessing of the Great One by accepting for you that you are a god, and for all the peace and forgetfulness of the past, that you may accept the Christ Power within you; for man knowingly started his involution into dense matter and he is now evolving out of dense matter.

To attain his **Mastership, his Godhood, here is a good Rule of Thumb:**

> Set your face to the Sun
> Never run
> Use spear of **Mind**
> Which is thought
> To stop what negativity has been wrought.
> Be a Brother
> Help another

Go in Peace And Use the Golden Force!

The Way of The Son of Man

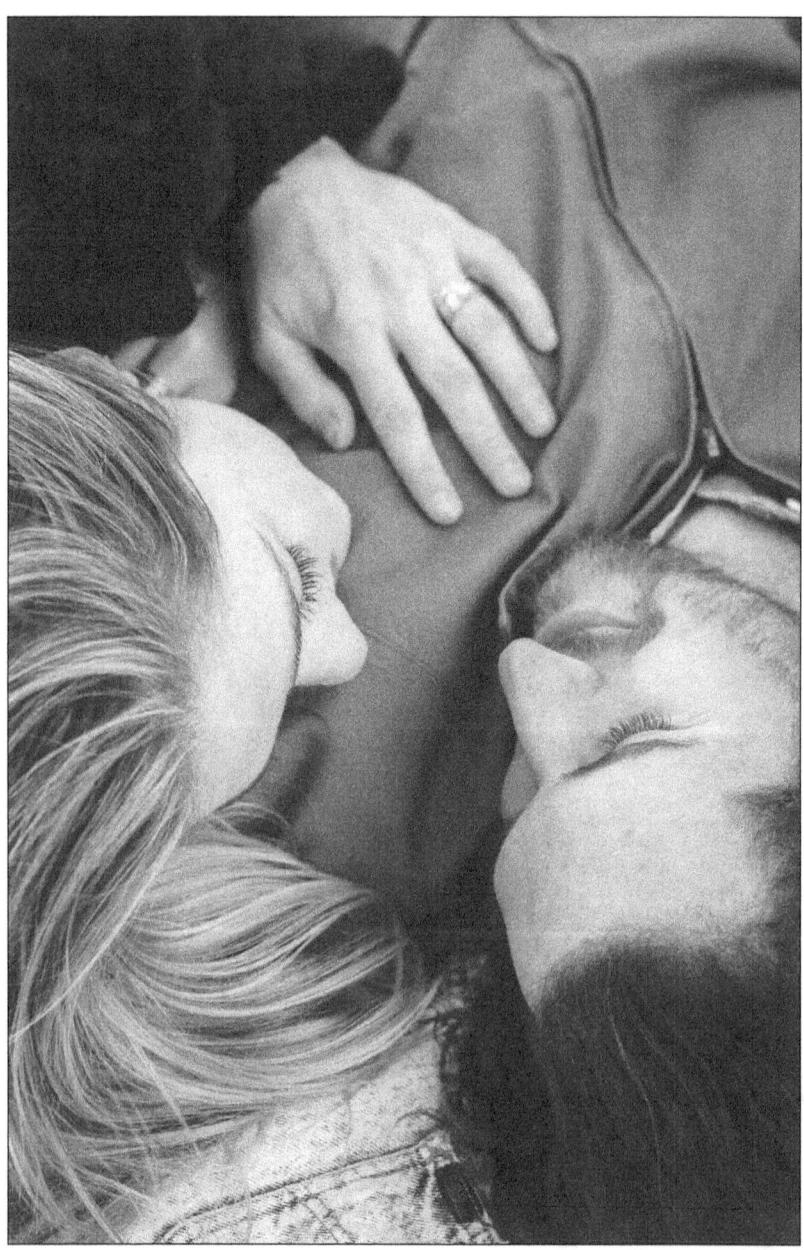

Neonbrand/Unsplash

Chapter 10

THE OCEAN OF SEX: GOD–MAN–WOMAN

The subject most talked about, the subject as spoken of by the popular writers, is the **"Eternal Triangle"** or should we say, the most misunderstood of all relationships? The thing I am trying to understand is, why call it the "eternal triangle," when we have just man and woman—or do we have a third? Who could the third person be? For it takes three points to make a triangle—could it be the **third point is the Great Creative Power, God?**

If this is true—and I am intuitively guided to say this, because without this creative force in our bodies, both psychic and physical, there would be no offspring and sexual intercourse would be an impossibility. In the first place, physical intercourse depends on feeling, and all the senses in the physical body which require the function of the psychic body.

With this taken into consideration, is it a wonder we have so much divorce? You see the truth is right in front of you all the time and you have never seen it. (You see it is necessary to have God in the triangle.) It is like most things taught in the Holy Bible or the Jewish Books. People do not pay any attention to what they are taught; they go blindly on and, anything which is not a piece of soap or a loaf of bread, they do not recognize, or understand. Certainly men and women should have recognized this by this time; the way they have fought and tried to possess one another has not attained one thing for either side of the fence. The fact of the matter is that there is never a way of doing anything except through the all-sure way of cooperation with the Father and one another. This is the way a successful business is run and this is the way that the Father set up this Universe, and cannot be changed and when one uses the **Law** as laid down by the Master Jesus and many other Great Masters, one is only working in cooperation with the Father, Who has and will guarantee to produce that which we choose.

The double triangle, as it represents a Universal principle in the function of things, should be of significance here. It is the number of the double triangle, which is two, which stands for the function of the Law of the triangle in action, on both the seen and unseen planes of action—in both worlds, in the physical world and the psychic world of God, as the Religionist would say it, but we say in these two spheres of vibration because it is really that way; sounds cold, doesn't it?

Just about this time I can hear you say to me: "Are you trying to tell me about a Great Creative Power that really works? You mean a real **God**?" It always causes dismay in me this wonder at a real God—for I am sure that I will never quite understand people that go to Church when they did not think that it is a real thing they are talking about—yes, it is a real **God**, a functioning **God**.

Cooperation is one thing, one word that if really understood will aid in bringing peace in this triangle, for there exists the idea of competition between the male and female, the basis of possessing and domination, which always leads to conflict. The only remedy for this is the real knowing of the complete function of God, man and woman; only through this can either of them, or both of them, obtain complete balance of the forces in their being.

Therefore, it is not a case of one or the other—either Man or Woman—running the other one, because as you will see if you finish this chapter, that one is just as dependent on the other for a full and happy life[1].

Do you feel that the creation of your body in your Mother's womb was a degrading thing? Then you are going to say, "Well, my mother and father were properly married." I am going to ask you, were they? You can still miss the most beautiful part of marriage if you do not understand.

Let us take the example of the common candle. It gives off light, but it also gives considerably more heat than light. Light is the direct function of a candle, heat the indirect, but we get more heat than light. A candle is a furnace adapted to the purpose of lighting. In order to give light, a candle must burn. Combustion is a necessary condition for receiving of light from a candle.

Therefore, it is impossible to ignore this combustion, but the same combustion gives heat. At first thought, it appears that the heat from the candle is spent unproductively; sometimes it is superfluous, unpleasant, annoying. If a room is lighted by candles, it will soon grow excessively hot; but the fact remains that light is received from a candle only because of combustion—by the development of heat and the incandescence of volatilized gases.

The same thing is true with the case of love and affection. To hold within one the great aspect of male/female—it is a great ocean, a mass aspect of the acceptance of God—of something of a common pattern of thought, with the flux and reflux within illuminated by God, the Teacher or Principle of Love, of Life trying to give Life to Love.

Therefore, the apparent physical sexual act is only the visible part of physical manifestation of the spiritual reality taking place—and to this most eyes and senses are dulled—so once again people see the gross or what they think is gross. Why do they think it gross? Because of the teachings of mass mind and their thinking that all there is, in and to the world, is what they See.

When you say to this beautiful lady, "I love you," in reality you are saying that you feel the Great God Force trying to pass from you to her. Is this obscene? Man, O Man, wake up to the eminency of the God you say you worship.

With the pulsing of this force, pressing on the bounds of the body, the glands are the points of conversion from the basic force of God to physical emotion—vibrating, swaying—emotional to the star-glint of the eye of all human beings when they feel the acceptance of the Love, or giving of the other—the other's (male or female) acceptance of the reflecting of Heaven and all Creation. How wonderful!

Scarcely a figure, male or female, approaches another, just to walk up to the other to talk, but that there will be a tremor travel across this great ocean which we call sex. Sex in the mind is a plane, so to speak, of function—not just visibly, but also invisibly, like a media or as you use a cell phone, it is a way to demonstrate God.

Man—Woman—God move across the face of the Moon—so on the edge of this great Ocean of Sex action, the glory of human form is faintly outlined under the trees of dense matter, or by the shore of soul. We then look into the deeps of the Great Creative God, for as we look into the star-glint eye of our lover, as well as the passioned fool who seeks a great God experience of Love, still maybe to the touch, to the approach, to the incantation of the eyes, of one shall burst forth uncontrollable, in that seething, rolling, engulfing—the wonderful but turbulent Ocean of Sex. Then comes the natural, visible demonstration—this ocean of sex and its millions and millions of tiny seed-like human forms contained within each person, the spheres of life—this, the mirror of the very Universe in which we live.

The Sacred Temple and innermost Holy Shrine of each body, where the life force produces Love—the Ocean of Sex flowing ever on through the great trunk and branches of humanity, from which, after all, you and you, the individual, only spring like a leaf-bud; the Ocean of Sex which we so wonderfully contain, and we are contained in—the Mind of the Universe, the Mind of God. When sometimes we feel and know this within, and identify ourselves with the Only, then do we understand that Love is something given, as something already understood and known.

Love and death—the two enigmas which confront us—the mystical man seems to be attracted by the face of death. It is because it has so many unknown avenues. It is a well-known psychological fact

The Ocean of Sex: God–Man–Woman

that in moments of powerful emotion, of great joy or great suffering, everything happening around about a man seems to him unreal, as a dream. This is the beginning of the Soul's awakening. When a man in dreams begins to be conscious of the fact that he is asleep and that what he sees is a dream, then he is waking up; this is like the moment of Love and Sex.

Love is only attained between two people when the male makes his declaration of love to her; the male then lets Her loose, thereby giving her up to the God she represents, and waits for the Female to come to him. This may sound contradictory to the social practice now used.

In the bird kingdom this is practiced, in the animal kingdom almost entirely. But let us see—say from a technical standpoint, in an electrical circuit the negative (-) pole, female, always flows to the positive (+) male. If it is right in physical matter, it is right in spirit. This same principle holds true in the working of the law.

This is the true pattern, because when he has declared his intentions, he has made a pattern, and then the two minds must meet in the God mind, which is One.

If you wish to be accepted by others, then you must accept others, and it must start with the ones closest to you, and the balancing force and power of the male aspect has been acquired; and remember if you are a male, this does not mean that the male aspect has been acquired or that you came into this life with it.

There is a potent aspect in the character of the male aspect, its nature; its action gives decision and knowingness of choice, its nature, which is one thing that a woman cannot develop, no matter how far along the Path—she needs this to use the God Force in its fullness of aspect this aspect is **authority**, and it is only transmitted through the male association.

Remember, God created **man** first, then **woman**. This does not make woman any less important, for **woman** gives **man** the love aspect of creation, for it was taken from man. The male is the creation of the **wo-man**, therefore it is necessary that Woman return to Man the Love He gave her, and it is a spiritual transfer, while the physical culmination of the physical intercourse is man's supreme giving to woman the power to create another being; and where no child is born, it is the release of power to woman's body, which converted, then she may create with mind. But without this she is like a virgin child, sweet and beautiful, but does not have any effect on the world around her.

On the other hand, woman releases to man *the "roundness of feeling,"* the softness of touch, both physical touch and the touch of word; in other words, the use of sound in communication. The feeling of the Rose Petal is the female aspect. The protection of a mother for her child against all danger, so the child will not be harmed, is what the male gave her when he passed the germ of life. This is the male aspect.

The **mass mind** of the female today is that when she mates, she is bestowing a favor on the male; this is not true. She is in reality fulfilling the requirements necessary for her own freedom.

Look about you, and all women that have become great in business, literary pursuits or professional pursuits have known the love and mating with the male of their choice, or have given birth to a child. Some have not, but always they have had the scepter of power passed to them by the male. If they did not, they have become warped and distorted in their dealings with other people. They are usually very envious people and completely self-centered.

In the case of the male, if he has not received the female or negative aspect of God, he is usually cold and hard, and he does not have the delicacy and kindness, love of beauty, personal relationship, friendship quality, and art and creative pursuits.

When the female turns her head up to her mate and parts her lips, she is accepting the male idiom of the spiritual aspect of the male, and whether the cycle is completed in the physical or not, she has opened the way for mental and physical stimuli to activate the Kundalini, and the uniting of the two atmospheres has taken place. This is the first step—the atmosphere of both male and female must be in resonance for the cycle to be completed.

In the uniting of the two electromagnetic fields—which is a means of conveyance of the two aspects of the God Force from whom these are given freely of one to the other, thus creating one uniform field—we have what might be said to take place when we say, "water will seek its own level;" then peace in the presence of God exists.

To you, *Man*, remember that when you have this woman in your arms (if she is following nature's plan) you are the source of everything—take her firmly but gently to you, think only of her. Give up completely to her happiness, then and only then will you reach the happiness you have been seeking.

To you, *Woman*, remember if you have any fear of this man, stay away from him, because you cannot "let go and let God;" you cannot admire and thrill to his every touch if you fear him or the mating. Do not think you can beat nature. No one ever has.

This is what the Great Creative Power of the Universe has ordained should be, and in this age, the New Age, the return of the Christ Force, this is what will be or man and woman will tear themselves apart.

There is a term which has been used by many, this is *"free love."* It is used to depict the ones who seeks just physical release alone, from any woman or source; but real *"free love"* is what we have to develop— the kind that is in the Universal pattern for the betterment of all man and womankind.

It is said that woman could stop all wars. It is rightly so, for if woman would accept her freedom in the sun with God and her mate, he would accept the female aspect which would not want to fight. Why? Because he would be at *peace*—peace within himself and not seeking that balance; and woman would be happy in the power of her divine freedom. Is this a matter of self-satisfaction, a case of self-gratification, a sensation of amusement? No, Not at all! Is your concept of sex a concept which is on the animal level? If so, then think of this; each must think and perform correctly.

The Golden Force

It makes no difference if you are following spiritual pursuits or a mundane material life, if you want the most out of life this is the way to acquire it.

We are now giving you a comparison of the two—Man and Woman—without prejudice, although I am a man writing this, because it was not I who created this Universe but the **Great Creative Power** which did the job, although I will admit many years ago I also tried to change the system.

To the female mass mind, freedom is doing what amuses her personally—what she accepts as pleasant and pleasing to her without any encumbrances of cooperation with another person, such as a mate. Occasionally she might like to have a man take her to the movies or for a little love affair, but not to have any strings attached.

There is nothing so pleasing to her as to fuss with her dress, her hair and adorn her body, as it is the body which she thinks is the main attraction.

This she wishes to do, to attract the male so that she can control him through his spiritual need and physical needs. Remember all things come from a spiritual stimulus, be they good or bad. She learns to control the male through stimulating his physical desire which is, too, both spiritual and physical; and then passes him by her refusals and keeps him dangling until her ego is satisfied, and unites with him only when she has reached the limits of his tolerance. Then she repeats this until she obsesses him and has complete control of him.

In this new age—the return of the Christ—for as surely as I sit here writing, the Christ is returning to earth more every day, but his is not a man. In this new age this cannot be, for the vibration of the earth's atmosphere is rising, therefore both male and female must have their freedom, both must be free to take their freedom and fill their place in the sun by carrying out the divine plan of theirs.

How can they gain their freedom? This can be attained by understanding their part in creation and marriage—marriage in a form where the raising of children is not the prime purpose, but first to know one another and their relation to the Creator.

The male is the bulwark for the female, for **he is mind**—the **female is emotion**[2]. This is the Mind, Primary Cause, the good Holy Bible says was created first.

The female, being Emotional Mind, should be a source of healing for children, and also for the adult males who are ill and in need of healing. If she wishes to function wholly, she should teach children, also teach woman about children and other subjects such as Philosophy and Science; and in order to do this she should have the male balance, for of him she gains the prerogative of power. Her female qualities will give her symmetry and beauty in other things; then, and then only will her real beauty appear, not only in character but in spirit of body and face.

If you want a thing or quality in yourself, then it is necessary to conform to the plan of creation—you also must be able to see this in other people. If you wish to be admired then you must admire others.

Then according to the Universal pattern, the female must go or flow to the male or positive in the material world, if she accepts him; otherwise he is forcing the issue, if he does as is practiced here on this earth at this time. The present Earth way of the Male keeping the Female so busy she cannot have choice or time to think is not right. Also, if a previous marriage has existed, regardless whether there has been legal divorce or not, even if both parties have been granted divorce, until a new marriage pattern is accepted by one or both of the parties, to a new mate, the divorced party is still giving mental acceptance to the marriage whether she or he hate their former mates or not.

Now when a new contract or pattern is mentally accepted by him or her, whichever the case may be—then all the reactions and thoughts of the former marriage will dissolve. Being mentally accepted, then they are married, license or no license, whether they live together or not.

For when there is peace in man's heart, there is peace in the world.

Then too does the Great Creative Power flow through both Man and Woman, and thus the triangle is formed with God, Man and Woman in this divine creation.

Notes:

[1] The major point of reference in understanding this chapter, as well as the entire book, is to think in terms of Power, Force and Energy. The Holy Order of MANS teaches that the soul is neither male nor female, but carries aspects of both. The soul chooses the gender of the physical body to develop certain qualities while incarnating: the male has a positive (or directive) physical body and a negative (or receptive) spiritual body, while the female has a negative (or receptive) physical body and a positive (or directive) spiritual body.

In this chapter the author describes the balancing of these two aspects through physical and spiritual intercourse, forming a complete circuit. One should think of oneself primarily as Soul/Self in search of experience, the gender of physical body a temporary thing that is discarded at transition.

[2] The term "emotion" is defined from the Latin: motion—to move; emotion—to move out, move away.

The Ocean of Sex: God–Man–Woman

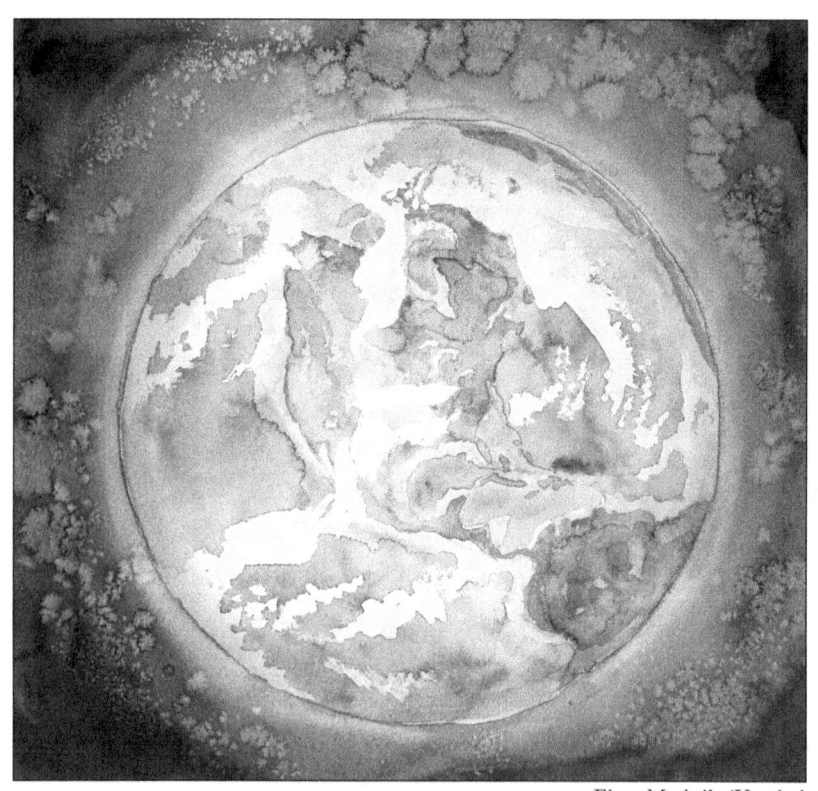

Elena Mozhvilo/Unsplash

Chapter 11
THE BLIND MAN SEES

Jesus said, "As a man thinketh, so is he"—a quotation which has been repeated many times by many kinds of religions and many philosophers. I say unto you, be not deceived by what you see with your physical eyes.

It is also said in the New Age, in these times, in the day of the return of the **Christ, those who see only what their half-blinded physical eyes do see, shall die**, as we call it, or pass-through transition.

If we think for a moment of the first statement, "As a man thinketh, so is he," then turn to the realization that all physical consciousness is based on knowledge and understanding taught to us as intellect: this is physical man's consciousness.

Seeing, then, takes an aspect or function of thinking, as the picture is built on the screen of our consciousness only. **Wisdom**, which is the function which involves spiritual sight and bringing to bear of our other five senses—this, of course, is the only true sight.

Man comes into this world through woman, and usually he brings with him the consciousness of the five physically functioning and five spiritually functioning senses; but as he starts to grow we start to impound into his consciousness that this thing is so, and that thing is so. Pretty soon, after a few years, we have unlearned him of all the truth he came into this world with, so that no longer is he able to hear and see with his spiritual eyes, but is ruled by mass mind, instead of by the God Mind as he should be, and then not only is he becoming educated—yes, **he is now educated to all the untruths**.

What a start he has now. It will take him many years to unlearn what he has been taught, so he may know the **Truth** and be **saved**, as the Christians call it. But actually it is letting the **God Force** flow through him again so that he may once again see, hear and feel in a true sense.

We have become so unthinking that only that which our physical seeing tells, this is the only reality we know. Until we have put God first, and reality or things of spirit. Reality is Cause of any experience, be it a thing of feeling or your pay check, and only comes from Mind of Spirit—or our part of it—as our minds are a part of the **Great Mind**.

Man is, the true man is, like a soldier in a steel tank where the only visual contact with the world around him is the optical sights and windows made of prisms built in the tank. He is gaining an experience in this state of vibration, which he could not experience except through the tank, likewise through his physical body or vehicle which protects him, the real him, very much like the man in the steel tank, it protects him from the attack of the enemy.

Think on yourself and all that is inside of you and place yourself at the center of being of your physical body, then look out at the world around you and see if the world around you does not look different, for at this time you will be in a place to take command of both the Ego and Will.

If you do this it will bring you a new concept of Life and we hope you will start and think. Think for your own good and many people around you, for don't forget that you are a broadcasting station and there are many receivers around you.

What do you want to build, happiness and success or hate, despair in your own family and the family next door?

For you are going to be in this physical body until you pass through transition at which time your sight will not be hindered with matter.

You will then function with your five spiritual senses "if" you are conscious of them when you go. You might not like what you see of the past.

Otherwise, you will be a long time, as a rule, getting to a place of self-control.

In this **Christ Day**, both physical and spiritual bodies will come together as one, and all things will be more and more vivid, more intensified. The emotions will react with more feeling and things which we did not feel concerned with ten years ago will be of the uttermost importance. These things would not have had then even a place in our thoughts; now we stop and consider them.

In this day, you must be doubly sure to have control of mind. The emotions and will are more violent—more unrest, more disease.

The Christ is returning now, now.

This force will eliminate all negation and disease. But, you say, look at the war, destruction and fear, death all around us—all of the negative thinking and thoughts.

Did you ever watch a man with a disease being treated when the Doctor gives him medicine? It is what he needs to produce a right and normal condition in his physical body. He will do what we call get better—get well. Then, all of a sudden, he will go through a crisis where he will appear to get worse or sicker than he was before. This is a natural pattern, because the needed medicine is breaking up the pattern of disease and then nature will take over. After the pattern is broken and the toxic materials are eliminated from the body and, as the Doctor would say, a pathological balance is reached, he then will feel better and symptoms will disappear, and he is said to be cured.

This is what is happening in the world today. This world is sick with fear and greed; the bloated Egos, all of the illness of our world civilization, all of the things that we see demonstrated in the individual lives around us are mostly a case of being misinformed and ignorant of the power that they possess. One of the outstanding reasons for this is that they are ignorant of the real ways taught by the Master Jesus. Because the so-called Christian Church has not taught the truth, the way of the Master and what he did in his life here. Churchmen are and have been influenced by the almighty dollar and have seen that the way to keep the people in slavery was to take out all of the teachings that referred to the **Law** so that the people would be totally dependent on the Church hierarchy.

Now the people at large are under the influence of **mass mind**, which is a dollar-conscious director of most movements. When it gets to the point that the people of misfortune in the streets are turned away when they come for help, then it is time we look and see what Church and how it performs, which our children go to. For I have known of more than one young man who was turned away by preachers or priests when they asked for help, not dollars, but spiritual help. One young man in a San Francisco jail, who later proved to be not guilty of the crime he was arrested for, asked me for a Priest. I personally called one twice and he never came to see the boy.

This is the time spoken of as the New Age or the Return of the Christ, and now the Christ Force is starting to break up the world pattern that man has made of materialism, and thus we see violence, death, war and many other things. The individuals are reacting to the healing of both mind and body as a person, as a nation, as a world which has been sick and is coming back to the Creator which made them, and all that is in the world of **God**.

Those that resist the Life Force, for there is life in all things—only in Man's consciousness does death exist—for death is the destroying element or action. If death existed as man depicts it, how could there be life?

God is everywhere, therefore, God would not destroy His own creation. Christ is the Son of God, so that Force of the Father through the Sun gives all life. Without life all things and persons and souls would not grow, for without life, there would be no action.

The Blind Man Sees

Without life to give action and desire of action or a yen for great and closer knowing of God, there would be no love of God, or love of Man by God. Also, the love of Man for one another is brought into manifestation only through acts between them.

The Christ Force is coming now in even greater force or intensity than it has. While man is planning to kill with atom bombs, and is testing these lethal weapons, man is also, even without war, raising the vibrations of the Earth's atmosphere and causing the expansion of the dense material matter, thus causing it to be less dense.

The expanding of matter will make and is now making it easier for the Christ Force to enter the atmosphere of Earth. You might say to me, well, this is good—yes, but not for those who have not mastered Self and Body.

This action will cause all kinds of violent reactions in those who do not understand and know God or the Golden Force.

Let me ask you, do you expect to see a man come down out of the sky when the Christ returns fully?

Do you pray just because you like to talk to the Golden Force—sounds pretty off-beat does it not? Well, you can become conscious of the Golden Force or Intelligence of the Solar System.

Just look back. Could you always read? Did you always read? Did you always know how to do Arithmetic? I think not.

Have you tried to know God as hard as you tried when you learned Arithmetic? What did you do when you learned the system of symbols of Arithmetic and how to work the symbols together through their laws?

Just so, it is also necessary to learn how to shut out mass mind thinking and to follow the laws of **God** in prayer. To know this is the method of raising the consciousness, it can be raised—**it can be**—so, too can the Law and its working with them be used consciously. This is when **God** comes first with **man**, and all other material things second.

In this, and through this **Christ Force** returning to Earth, the negative things, evil, death, fear, destruction, are exposed, but will disappear from the mass mind of Earth when they are put aside by each individual **person**. The first step is, get to know thyself. If man does not do this, the power and forces of this atmosphere will put him aside. He will be relieved of his physical body.

Get to know God.

The Blind Man Sees

Bradley Allweil/Unsplash

Chapter 12

CONSCIOUSNESS

This chapter might well be the first chapter, or it might be the last, for it is the first thing we should attempt to learn and attain, but it usually is the last.

It is the simplest yet one of the most complex, for it is the "Let go and let God" of all of it. It is the thing that we should have acquired in order to fully work the "Law of God."

If you don't want to think, don't bother to read this chapter.

We have talked of many things, the Law, the Electromagnetic fields of Man, our atmosphere that is Man's atmosphere. Mind and the relation of Man and Woman, the Way—all of the methods or principles are changeless, but their action and reaction in your life will bring new experiences day by day. They are ever-evolving through matter and effect of spirit. For all things are in constant motion.

We are evolving when we first sense the existence of a higher ideal state to that we are operating in. The ideal state of Matter is pure form. While Deity is the ideal state of Mind in matter that we call Spirit.

The purpose of matter, in its evolution, is wholly toward those forms created which will sustain the principles of Life—while in the higher forms of the bodies, matter thus gains a higher consciousness— that of the chemistry of Life. Matter always evolves with the beings using it and the use of it.

This is because the body is the living vehicle of the Soul. It sustains and manifests consciousness.

With this, you can say man's consciousness is aspiring to a higher consciousness or Cosmic Consciousness—which is the same as saying that man is aspiring to become conscious of this Universe as a whole.

This includes Matter, this world, other worlds, the psychic realm of the Souls which have gone beyond material sight, and all cycles of Life—it is the blending of our individual part of the Great Mind with the Mind of God, the Great Creative Intelligence and the Self becoming unified with Life as a whole, that is, the Life principle or Christ principle.

Then the desires of material achievement are dwarfed to the point that selflessness becomes a reality. This is the union with God and Christ.

Remember, matter is an aspect of Life, and the same Life is a motivator and part of Mind. It is continuous through both, although through all creation we have Life and Mind as the two polarities of our consciousness.

Whenever Life develops a cell, it develops a Mind concept and the multiplicity of these concepts are a reflection of the Master Mind of the unit, be it Man or substance. Therefore, we are God to the cells of our bodies. These are life cells.

Life of the body receives and transforms matter through the digestive system. Therefore, all of the energies received are transformed in essence. These energies are used by the brain and other cells in general—for thinking, no matter on what level this may be, good or bad.

Mind and body are the two aspects of Life—are capable of modifying the vibration of Spirit, as Jesus, said, "As a man thinketh, so is he," also a man is what he eats.

In the scheme of nature, from the highest form of intelligence to the lowest, in the use of the word *form*, we mean the form, shape, the matrix or structure—in the second use of the word *form*, we are using the word in a collective manner, a group or category. This is a very important part of understanding.

Life demonstrates the pronounced ability for a precise memory; all molecules and atoms have patterns of memory and function. In using the word *Life*, we are not talking of an abstract objective thing or something which is not real. This is an actual force in action and is an essential part of our existence in the **now**. It is the Savior of Man.

Life is the Father Force through the Sun/Son of God. Life drives out negation and what you call death. *It is the Christ descending to Earth or coming into the solid form of matter.*

Let us go back to the memory patterns of the function of various forms.

Consciousness sorts out vibrations and puts them with associated vibrations, differences, contrast to one another, thus bringing order out of chaos. Thus, we have sensations or thought, and they sense or record for future use.

Thus Mind can create matter, if the consciousness of the function is present.

This is why, when a person thinks only of material things, it sets up a rhythm of action and reaction, which excludes the basic Life principle and death occurs to the person or form of function. Thus also the death of ideals or mental normal function is bound to take place. It is well to always keep the three **L's** in front of our mind at all times, if we are to attain any degree of the higher Life:

Life—Light—Love

On the material plane:

Christ—Force—Action

The effect of vibrations sets up the consciousness and stimulates and constitutes thinking, this thing of action and reaction or the positive and negative impulses. Their influences in our living is again the things which come into our Universe and what will happen in our life.

Today, physical scientific research men are always probing and thinking in what they call the unknown worlds, both the microcosm and macrocosm. Why the probing?

What are these realms—why the search for the things they do not know exist in the **now**? They are developing **consciousness**.

Aspiration and inspiration are the aspects, which are fired by the imagination, and the imagination rises to its height or level of sensitivity to the point in accordance with the impressions it receives; these are the active principles of creating.

Consciousness comes from the Soul, or comes from the mental aspect of Life Force—thinking, sensation—these motivations are the active principles of imagination and its aspects.

With Cosmic Consciousness we understand and sympathize, we are one with it, whatever it may be. Intellect alone is not enough. We know, we feel, **we are one with it**. The man, the horse, an all-embracing idea of the way, the God, or the life of all mankind.

Man know thy Self—also Brother Man and all nature will be revealed through thy Cosmic Consciousness.

Man's life has its meeting point between the seen material and the unseen world or Cosmic All-ness; **Here is consciousness** and he who is open to it may at this moment or that moment foresee this future.

Why? Because we do not have existence, except as of this moment ever-passing into the new moment. Imagination with experience permits consciousness to anticipate the future.

Therefore the real reason for the development of Consciousness is the attainment of knowledge. In cases where memory goes back a long way—imagination as the activator foresees far into the future.

This happens where memory and imagination are correlated with the Life principle or Christ, God the Father is the Mind of all minds, and is the power on which all of this works.

Imagination is not just realizing an image. This would be a limitation. It is the power or force generated by an image—the concept or reactions, which have emanated from the image. For it is through imagination more than memory that one can get to realize one's Self.

We should ever work toward and realize an absence of fear or evil intent, this then will not clutter up our memory.

Choose fear and you have ignorance.

Nothing is more free than the imagination of Man, although it cannot exceed that original stock of ideas furnished by the internal and external senses, except in the event that you free yourself of the external influences and realize that you are a Universe to your-Self. This you can do through the Law of Epigenesis, which is just the outgrowth of Cause and Effect. For the more you put in the more you can get out.

Imagination is the everything of this moment in your life and mine. It is the command for action or the alchemist of power. It is the key to the gates of Heaven and the Aladdin's lamp in the lower or secondary action, in the use of the Law.

The magic arts are only workable by and through pure and intense and powerful imagination on the highest level man can operate here on earth. Be they good or bad.

The man that is aware or has an awakened consciousness realizes and is conscious of the constant change in conditions, for nothing is stationary. This is also the becoming—the Epigenesis in action—the evolving of force or vector curve.

As a solar system moves majestically through space in what a man would say eons of time, but in reality only in the now, so, too, does man move through the Path of the Law, be he bad—or good—as you say, but I say there is no **bad**, for all would evolve or retrograde to the original form of the Master Idea of Creation on the way of the Christ in the **Cross** of Calvary. So too does Man follow the Cross of the positive and negative to heaven or nothingness.

Can you conceive of a mind that is still—except for an instant, an interval time? Even when we do what we call being still and opening up the channel for Infinite Mind to come through us, here again we are under a controlled pattern of mind control.

Every cell is constantly breaking down and building up; this is what we might call perfect balance.

Not thought—but Consciousness, is the prime factor of your development and the path to becoming the God-like Man.

Christ healed his Consciousness of the imperfections—to the perfections of the **Law**.

Mind is the spiritual organ of the being, with absolute perfection at its highest level.

A stationary condition does not exist in an awakened Consciousness. All things are in motion; it may work on only one image at a time.

When we gain control of thinking, then our mental responses to various rates of vibrations are acute, then we are what is usually called becoming sensitive, then we can see, hear, know, and both material and spiritual life becomes one. We might say we are living in the midst of spirituality, because all is one basic energy.

When one awakens spiritually then he can truly say, "My brother" for he will know and feel the reason why. If one is a thinker, he has a greater horizon and is not **limited**.

The Holiness (wholeness of all things) breaks onto his consciousness as a golden dawn—he is no longer alone.

Intellect is the resultant of the sense, and our sentiment is the result of our emotion.

The finite mind is that which only becomes active through passive use; through limitation it may reach the absolute. It must receive matter in order to act and fashion into form that which is being created.

That which is real to man is that which he can realize through his senses, regardless of whether it is actual or real.

Man must be Conscious of other forms of living before he can realize himself or them. Mind is not the brain. It is not located in any one part of the body, but it exists in all parts of the body. For as you already know, Mind and Life are the integral parts of Consciousness; likewise, the Mind is the next to Godliness of man, but not his Soul.

Mind is the basic all-pervading pattern of all existence. Therefore, the intelligence of a Man is the sum total of the intelligence of all the atoms of which he is made. We can draw only one conclusion from that: a constantly sick man is not very intelligent.

Noise and sound are not actually in existence until they are realized.

A Guide Rule:

Always question a reality or thing you sense—it may not be actually true. Always question your mental interpretations of what thing is real.

To understand the true interpretation of sensation is to acquire a high state of consciousness and control.

Remember the Creative Power is in you now.

REFLECTION

God of our Fathers, God of All,
Ageless God that manifests in the short and tall,
Ageless winds, that caress my cheeks,
Whisper a message of the God I seek.

No matter where I look, I find
A lot of God, a little of me
In the mirror, or the lonely tree
For where He is, I must be
Because God is all there is of me.

Roland Cousins/Unsplash

Chapter 13
HOW MUCH DO YOU SEE?

Let me bring to your attention once again that all we see is that which the other thing radiates, the light or vibration which comes from it, it might be a person, an object, a light, the things of the material world—this is the seeing with the physical eyes. These must also be, when collected in form in the consciousness, a thing which is in our consciousness or we will probably not see it at all.

It has been recognized for a long time by men of science that vibrations give forth impressions, but their findings are not always explainable with the present research approaches. The medical doctor and experts in their fields take the symptoms of disease to find the cause. In their thinking, it is the germ. In other words, they have disregarded laws and words. They have disregarded laws and principles which will explain the cause.

The method of repetition in experiments leads to many general scientific principles, or what is taken as accepted principles. To explain this, if a certain test is repeated a number of times with the same thinking as a basis and the same results obtained, then this is supposed to be a sound basis on which to base a hypothesis or supposition.

They fail to realize that truth, a basic truth of this Universe, that the material and spiritual are not a multitude of separate things; it is all one—**One Mind**. When one has been thinking about one mind—all things as one for a period of time, he finds missing parts for the purpose of finding the cause which must exist.

The Golden Force

Now, if we will but think: that all matter is a state of vibration, and that it is not solid matter as perceived by the physical eye and realized by our brother scientists. Let us know that it is only vibration that we sense—for seeing is sensing—we are then taking the first step to true consciousness of the Universe we live in. Then and only then can we really understand how the Master Jesus was able and how we too can heal, if we start to be conscious of the world we live in. This is a true scientific approach.

Let us think what have you often said? "I know a thing exists because I see it" or the real oldie, "I will believe it when I see it."

What do you mean, "I see it?"—this is unscientific. When you sense it, yes, that is correct. Personally, "I mean that I see It"—in other words my consciousness, at this point of understanding of consciousness, "It sees it." I do not mean my physical body or brain or eyes; I mean my consciousness is conscious of its presence.

The word see as given by Webster defines it to mean "get knowledge through the eye." This definition alone tells how inadequate the process is. Now, just for your own information, search the internet for a book or article which gives you, in simple language, how the eyes function and their accuracy before the received image is recorded and reconstructed in the mind for the recognition of consciousness.

Anyone can test, or have tested, his eyes by instruments, but our tasting, smelling or feeling the things we think we see—that is different, but are we sure these senses are dependable? For example, have we not all had dreams at night in which things, houses, people or animals were pictured and appeared to be very real, to have life and color, form, just as material things do when we are in what we call an awakened state? I personally would not say that they always exist, but from one aspect they do: sometimes we have impressions in other senses, which tell us so.

Let us go back and restate our former statement. Instead of saying, "I know a thing exists because I see it," let us say, "When we see a thing while awake, it is not the thing itself which our consciousness realizes, but a picture of it."

How Much Do You See?

If a blind man looks toward a room of people and does not see them, does this prove the people are not there? The picture vibration made upon the retina of every eye will be the same whether it is consciously observed or not.

It is the vibration picture which is conveyed to my consciousness and produces the picture through the optic nerve and brain. This is all the consciousness can work with, except the spiritual senses.

If you will study how a motion picture camera and projector functions, how frame after frame of pictures (that is individual pictures) are thrown on the screen—in fact 16 frames a second—this gives life-like reproduction just as does the continual change of vibration radiated from the numerous objects conveyed through the lens of the eye to the cornea (which is composed of tiny structures called rods and cones, which react to the chemical interchange). As impulses are sent through the optical nerves to the brain, they reform in consciousness of mind.

The scientist will tell you it is light, but light is only vibration. Thus we see, it was vibration we saw, not the thing we thought we saw.

What happens if other vibrations interfere with the vibrations coming from the thing we are looking at? Well, the thing will change in appearance to you. Will the thing change? No. The thing will not change, but our picture on our consciousness will.

Even the persons themselves can influence what they will see, and their conscious picture will not be like the thing they are looking at in every detail.

There is one exception and that is when man is able to see with his spiritual eyes, that we will speak of later.

This is spoken of in Isaiah 42:20: "He sees many things but does not observe them: his ears are open but he does not hear."

The fact that the vibration of light passes through the lens of the eye and is picked up on the retina: put yourself, in your mind, in the theater looking at a picture on the screen. This is like sitting in the eye—in front of the retina and behind the lens. The screen would be the lens of the eye; you would not know what was going on outside the body—only what you saw through the lens of the eye.

The retina is a curved surface, with thousands of tiny structures called rods and cones per every 1/4 inch. These are connected to tiny nerves, which lead to the optic nerve. The tiny fibers come together in a heavy cord, like the form of a string, which is the optic nerve that goes to the brain. Here the picture is recreated in consciousness.

About this time, you are wondering why the long detail of how the eyes function, and you are saying, "I am not going to become a doctor, that is their business." My answer to you is that you know so little about yourself and you are so..o..o, so..o..o cock-sure of what is so, and not so, I hoped to show you that you are in a dangerous place and it is time to stop and say, "Maybe I don't know so much as I thought I did." Then again, "It is possible there is more to the world I live in than I thought there was."

Remember, **you are inside of this vehicle looking out!** How do you **know** what you are doing? Answer: **Consciousness**. There you sit in the darkened chamber of your inner being and most of you are still **blind**.

Let us go back to function. In other words, the picture vibrations are transmitted to the brain by electrical impulses or vibrations. A myriad of interrupted vibrations are the conveying means of getting the picture from the outside to the brain. This is true, but where, how, some of the details of nerves, energies and where they come from have been omitted here.

The vibrations stimulate certain brain nerve centers; consciousness is the translator of these into the pictures.

What of all the abnormal atomic energy in the air and the strange music we hear around us—is not this affecting the pictures we see? What about the added energies from the Son of God? It is more or less in the last sixty years that telepathy has been accepted by science.

Really, when we do not have full knowledge of a body process, our seeing it does not prove anything to us. Even after experiments that we have, a certain picture in consciousness does not prove that the thing really exists as we believe it to be.

It is, therefore, a fact that the images we see of conditions, dreams, things we do not understand, tire us from a physical standpoint. Yet, they may be real to us as individuals.

This we have spoken of is another proof that the one that aspires to know God should not permit himself to be affected by the materialistic viewpoint, thus becoming entangled in difficult situations.

It is true. Scientific men as a group in the past have had many false theories, which have been accepted as basic truth and taught. These now are being retracted: for instance, the theory on Ether.

The evidence that science was fooled by accepting what they saw, heard, felt physically—should at least start people to open their eyes. Let it be said here that I believe in a scientific approach, and I do. But I also believe in a complete scientific approach.

There is one thing that all people can learn above all else from the scientific man. **He has stick-to-it-ness.** This is what the Christians and others lack today—so many thousands sway with the wind.

Don't be a Do-Nothing about your future.

For you have millions of years if you follow the ways of the **Creator**—I did not say a **dogma**.

You cannot stand still—if you do **you will disintegrate**. The Way of the Masters of all time is so beautiful, and an exciting **way to live**.

We have said that you cannot believe all you see and this is a fact, for in the case of the Ether theory, it was a case of pure rationalization and a way to deny the force of the Creative Mind of God.

One may ask the question, "Do I really exist?" My answer: "Not the way you think you do." This is my answer to this question and always will be.

Fellow seekers, open your eyes and relate the truth and discuss the questions you have in your Mind with others. Do not be afraid.

Maybe the man next door also has things he wishes to talk about. Work with your neighbor, and you will get more answers to all of life's problems. All problems are in the same group. They are all of what you call a spiritual group.

Music is vibration and it is in the sound spectrum. Music, as well we all know, is a soul-stirring thing. There is nothing greater to bring peace and contentment, or to raise us to action, as the vibration of music. Of course, you cannot see the vibration of music with the physical sight, which is what most people live with.

Music is the material manifestation of vibration and is composed of the same energy as the vibration of matter.

Music first arouses the mind into realization, and brings certain psychic forces into action. The action is felt all through the body.

You can feel the beat of the drum, the shrill call of the flute and the notes of the piano in the solar plexus of the body.

Some music makes you feel warm all over. Some sets every nerve to tingling. You cannot see anything coming from the flute or piano. Yet, even with our eyes closed, we hear—feel—and there is still another sensation, which is the response of the mind.

We all know that light is faster than sound and that some music has a higher frequency than others. This is the difference in the sensation.

If you are interested in God, you are interested in light and sound, for they are manifestations of Spirit. Vibration is the phenomenon, which is existent in light, sound and thought. Vibration is a means of healing.

Vibration is the means of feeding
Soul—Spirit—Mind—Body

Is there a soul so dead who never to
    Himself has said,
Where is this land I go to now?

Where is this place called heaven?

Or is this all a hoax, an advertising idea
   Perhaps just a stunt on the human race—
Maybe I am not I at all,
   Or is the race riding for a fall?

No, it is not a stunt. But the people of the race have been held in slavery by not being taught to think, see and hear.

Learn to see, and all other God-given faculties are the same as learning to play an instrument. We use the finger exercises to create a dexterity of movements with fingers, and coordinate these with the eyes seeing the notes on the paper. It is so that the finger will express not only the notes, but the feelings that come from within, the gaining of new consciousness.

It is a fact the musician senses a melody, which is not on paper.

The life you lead can be affected in only one way—man's realization of what actually exists **now**—by his **interpretation**. For, from baby to ancient sage, we are constantly changing our realization of things.

To me, to my consciousness, the seen and unseen must blend for it to be true.

For as we get closer to God, we get closer to actual truth.

So, let us start the next chapter of our **Life** with a clear mind, a love of Creation, at least a desire to know the **Truth** and what actually is, whether it hurts or not.

Let us not be afraid of accepting the Holy Bible and Science of Technology together. For it is not sacrilegious for us to want an all-encompassing **God** as It is. Expand your consciousness, and know your God and His solar system by knowing yourself.

Peace cometh, as Peace is.

The Golden Force

About the Author
Rt. Rev. Earl W. Blighton, D.D.

There are master teachers, mystics, healers, and gurus, but the Adept is a special class of spiritual master that combines the skills and qualifications of these and supersedes them all. Earl W. Blighton was an Adept. Acknowledged by some of the leading spiritual teachers of his day, including the Sufi Master Murshid Samuel Lewis, Theosophist Joe Miller, and the Hindu leader Satguru Subramuniyaswami, Blighton was widely regarded as a leader and principal in the burgeoning spiritual movement of the 1960's. His favorite saying was "By their fruits ye shall know them."

As founder of the Holy Order of MANS, a group that epitomized Christian Mysticism and the Occult Philosophies of Rosicrucianism and Theosophy, Blighton proved that he could indeed produce "fruits." He did it by teaching from his heart, by which he attracted scores of young people who then mirrored what he taught in their lives. Blighton was called Father Paul by his students.

In five years, the Holy Order of MANS had over three thousand members, and Brother/Sister houses on two continents. Blighton showed how spiritual development could be accomplished not in decades but in a few short years. His writings and oral teachings still

The Golden Force

live on through those who met him, and by those who have discovered and been inspired by his work.

His lectures, writings, and the Holy Order of MANS Curriculum are available on the website www.HolyOrderOfMANS.org.

A calendar of Zoom classes and in-person Order events are at the website www.HolyOrderOfMANS.com.

www.ingramcontent.com/pod-product-compliance
Lightning Source LLC
Chambersburg PA
CBHW050252120526
44590CB00016B/2314